## ASA Special Series

VOLUME 50

*Introduction*

The Swiss Arbitration Association (ASA, Association suisse de l'arbitrage) is Switzerland's leading arbitration organization. With more than a thousand members, it brings together the world's most eminent arbitration practitioners from six continents and 50+ jurisdictions.

Since its foundation in 1974, ASA helps shape the development of international arbitration for the benefit of users worldwide. Its signature Annual Conferences in Zurich and Geneva explore topical issues with high-calibre experts from all over the world. The papers and materials are subsequently published in the ASA Special Series.

*Editors*

Each volume of the ASA Special Series is edited by different editors from among the ASA members and who have been the (co-)organizers of the pertinent ASA Annual Conference or are specialists in a particular topical issue to which a volume is dedicated.

*Objective*

The ASA Special Series are published to foster innovation in and to promote international arbitration globally.

They contain the full edited versions of the papers of the ASA Annual Conferences as well as ad hoc arbitration brochures published by ASA.

*Frequency*

One to two volumes per year, with one volume typically published following the ASA Annual Conference.

*The titles published in this series are listed at the end of this volume.*

# ESG and Disputes

## Flash in the Pan or Game Changer?

Edited by

Urs Weber-Stecher
James Menz

Wolters Kluwer

*Published by:*
Kluwer Law International B.V.
PO Box 316
2400 AH Alphen aan den Rijn
The Netherlands
E-mail: lrs-sales@wolterskluwer.com
Website: www.wolterskluwer.com/en/solutions/kluwerlawinternational

*Sold and distributed by:*
Wolters Kluwer Legal & Regulatory U.S.
920 Links Avenue
Landisville, PA 17538
United States of America
E-mail: customer.service@wolterskluwer.com

ISBN 978-94-035-4068-9

e-Book: ISBN 978-94-035-4078-8
web-PDF: ISBN 978-94-035-4088-7

# Editors

**James Menz** is a founding partner of rothorn legal. With over fifteen years of experience, his practice focuses on complex disputes in the construction, engineering, energy, transportation, pharmaceutical, and biotechnology sectors. He has acted as counsel, arbitrator, and arbitral secretary in dozens of proceedings under a variety of applicable institutional rules and substantive laws. Most recently, Mr Menz worked in-house as a senior litigation expert for Bombardier Transportation, managing a range of domestic and international project and construction litigations and arbitrations and advising the business on dispute avoidance and resolution strategies. From 2016 to 2018, Mr Menz was Deputy Secretary General and Head of Case Management at the German Arbitration Institute (DIS), where he supervised hundreds of arbitration and ADR proceedings and served on the drafting committee for the revised 2018 DIS Arbitration Rules. Previously, for over ten years, Mr Menz practised international arbitration, litigation, and competition law with major law firms in New York and Zurich. A graduate of the George Washington University Law School and admitted to the New York Bar, Mr Menz regularly sits as an arbitrator and publishes and speaks on issues in international commercial arbitration.

**Urs Weber-Stecher** is an independent Swiss arbitrator and mediator with over twenty-five years of experience in dispute resolution. He has acted as party representative and arbitrator in numerous international and national arbitrations in various industries and as a mediator in several commercial disputes. Before starting his practice as a solo practitioner, he was partner and head of the arbitration team in a commercial law firm in Zurich for almost twenty years. In his mediation practice, Urs Weber-Stecher draws on his many years of experience in contract and settlement negotiations. The combination with specific mediation techniques allows him to assist the disputing parties with empathy and competence in their settlement process. Until a few years ago, antitrust law was another area in which Urs Weber-Stecher regularly advised companies and represented them before the authorities. Before joining a law firm, Urs Weber-Stecher worked for several years at the Federal Office for Foreign

Economic Affairs (now part of SECO) and was a member of Switzerland's diplomatic team for negotiations on a multilateral agreement on investment under the OECD and a member of the negotiating team for bilateral investment treaties.

# Contributors

**Leonardo Conte** is a research assistant at The Swiss Institute for Alternative Thinking and PhD candidate in Economic and Social Sciences at the University of Fribourg, Switzerland. Former Research Fellow of the Harvard Policy and Institutional Research Project, he is co-founder of Rethinking Economics Switzerland and an adjunct professor of Economics at Franklin University Switzerland. His interdisciplinary background in behavioural economics and consumer culture informs his research interests in pluralist economics, qualitative research, and sustainable consumption.

**Lucy Greenwood** is an independent arbitrator specializing in international commercial and investment disputes. She has practised international arbitration since 1998 (in London, Paris and Houston) and has acted as an arbitrator in more than ninety arbitrations since becoming a full-time arbitrator in 2017. She is highly regarded for her prompt, efficient resolution of disputes and active case management of arbitrations and is particularly in demand as a chair for major energy disputes. She is ranked Band 1 by *Chambers* as a Global Elite Thought Leader by *Who's Who Arbitration* and was shortlisted by *Legal 500* for Arbitrator of the Year in 2023. Lucy is a Chartered Arbitrator, a Texas attorney and a Solicitor of the Senior Courts of England and Wales. She is a Trustee of the Chartered Institute of Arbitrators, Past Chair of the International Committee, Dispute Resolution Section, American Bar Association, Past Chair of the North America Branch of the Chartered Institute of Arbitrators and a Fellow of the College of Commercial Arbitrators. She is the founder of the Campaign for Greener Arbitrations, an initiative to reduce the environmental impact of international arbitrations. More information is available at www.greenwoodarbitration.com.

**Jackie van Haersolte-van Hof** has been the Director General of the LCIA since 1 July 2014. She regularly sits as an arbitrator and has handled cases under the ICC, LCIA and UNCITRAL Rules, as well as those of the Netherlands Arbitration Institute (NAI) and UNUM. She is on the ICSID roster of arbitrators and was and is a member of several ICSID Annulment Committees, including as President. She is a professor of civil law, in particular arbitration law, at Leiden University and a member of GAR's editorial board. Previously, she practised as counsel and arbitrator in The Hague at her GAR 100 boutique HaersolteHof, which she set up in 2008 after three years as counsel in the international arbitration group at Freshfields Bruckhaus Deringer in Amsterdam. Before that, she was at De Brauw Blackstone Westbroek and Loeff Claeys Verbeke.

**Sunny Kapoor** is a Counsel at Clifford Chance Frankfurt and a member of the commercial litigation and arbitration team. He represents clients in complex cross-border and domestic disputes, particularly in the areas of banking and finance, real estate and automotive, with a focus on mass claims. Sunny currently represents and advises clients in high-profile climate change disputes. He also acts as an arbitrator and regularly publishes and speaks on current legal topics, including climate change-related issues. Sunny is a lecturer at the Goethe University in Frankfurt am Main and a founding member of the Frankfurt Disputes Circle.

**Moritz Keller** is an arbitration partner in the Frankfurt office of Clifford Chance. He represents clients in both commercial arbitration and investment arbitration proceedings under the ICSID, ICC, UNCITRAL, DIS, Swiss Rules, Austrian Chamber, and many other arbitration rules. Moritz regularly deals with matters both under public international law and a variety of domestic laws. Focal points of his practice are the energy, infrastructure, construction, and banking sectors. He has also been instructed recently in several high-profile climate change disputes. Moritz is a member of several arbitration institutions and sits on the ICC Commission on Arbitration and ADR, as well as the ICC Commission on Energy and the Environment. He acts as an arbitrator and is an accredited mediator on the Energy Community Panel of Mediators. Moritz is part of the law faculties of the Universities of Frankfurt am Main and Passau (Germany), where he regularly lectures on matters of investment arbitration and EU law. He frequently publishes on a variety of subjects within his expertise, most recently as author and editor of a commentary on CETA and EU Investment Protection Law.

**Professor Crenguta Leaua**, PhD habilitatus, is teaching comparative international arbitration, business law and communications and new technologies law at the Bucharest University of Economic Studies, Faculty of Law and Faculty of Cybernetics and Informatics in Economics. Recognized as a thought leader in international dispute resolution and founder of LDDP-Bucharest, she is a past vice-president of the International Court of Arbitration of the International Chamber of Commerce ICC Paris and a member of the board of directors of the Silicon Valley Arbitration and Mediation Center. She is a correspondent member of UNIDROIT (Rome) and an expert in technology-related international disputes at UNCITRAL. She is currently integrating her legal expertise in dispute avoidance and resolution at the crossroads between law, economics, psychology and technology, developing the alternative thinking method, as director of The Swiss Institute for Alternative Thinking.

**Florian Mohs** is a partner of Pestalozzi's Litigation & Arbitration Group in Zurich. He represents clients as counsel in international commercial arbitrations, in court proceedings in Switzerland as well as in negotiations and mediations; he also acts as arbitrator and Swiss law expert. Florian handles a wide range of commercial and corporate disputes, having broad experience in advising industrial companies in engineering and construction disputes, trading companies in commodities disputes, and pharmaceutical companies in licensing matters. Admitted to the Swiss Bar; trained in both civil (Switzerland and Germany) and common law jurisdictions (New Zealand); expert on the CISG.

**Alison Pearsall** is the Group Head of Litigation, Dispute Resolution & Risk Management at Eviden International. She has extensive experience advising multinational corporations on high-value/risk arbitration and litigation cases in the energy, IT, waste, and water sectors. Prior to her in-house career, she exercised in private practice in New York and Paris, specializing in international arbitration and complex commercial litigation. She previously served as the Common Law Counsel at the ICC International Court of Arbitration. She is currently a member of the ICC Commission on Arbitration and ADR and previously served as a court member of the London Court of International Arbitration and Chair of the New York City Bar Committee on International Trade. Alison is qualified both as a US attorney and as a mediator.

**Isabelle Romy** is a partner with the law firm Kellerhals Carrard in Zurich, and her practice focuses on international litigation, arbitration and private international law in commercial matters. Isabelle is also a recognized expert in environmental law, including climate law and construction law in Switzerland, and regularly advises private companies and public bodies in these fields, including in environmental litigation. She co-heads KC's ESG & Sustainability Desk, which was launched in 2023. Isabelle has also been a professor at the University of Fribourg and the École Polytechnique Fédérale de Lausanne since 1996, as well as a member of the SIX Swiss Exchange Sanction Commission since 2001 and Vice-Chairwoman since 2008. From 2003 to 2008, she was a deputy judge at the Swiss Federal Supreme Court. Isabelle Romy sits on the Board of Directors of several Swiss companies and was a member of the Board of Directors of UBS AG and UBS Group AG from 2012 to 2020.

**Samantha J. Rowe** is a partner in Debevoise & Plimpton's International Dispute Resolution and Public International Law Groups and co-leads the firm's ESG Group. Ms Rowe has represented private clients, States and State-owned entities across multiple jurisdictions in arbitrations and litigations before domestic and international courts and tribunals, governed by various substantive laws and conducted under the rules of the ICC, LCIA, ICSID, UNCITRAL and SIAC. Ms Rowe has been named to The Lawyer's Hot 100 list, which recognizes the profession's most innovative and inspirational lawyers. The magazine noted the 'precedent-setting cases' she advises on. She was also named a Rising Star for international arbitration by Law360, a UK Rising Star, and a Rising Star in the Commercial Arbitration practice category at the inaugural Euromoney Legal Media Group Europe Rising Stars Awards. Ms Rowe is included in *The Legal 500's* International Arbitration Powerlist, and she is listed by *Who's Who Legal* (2022) as a leading lawyer and thought leader for arbitration. *Chambers Global* (2024), *Chambers UK* (2024) and *The Legal 500 UK* (2024) recommend her for International Arbitration, with the guides noting that she is 'an excellent lawyer with a clarity and expression of thought that enables complex matters to be understood quickly.' She is said to be 'everything that you would ever want in a lawyer,' 'extremely professional and knowledgeable', and a 'brilliant advocate'. Ms Rowe is a solicitor advocate of the Senior Courts of England & Wales and is admitted to the New York Bar.

**Patrick Thieffry** is an independent arbitrator consultant, mainly in construction, infrastructure, environmental and energy-related matters. A member of the Paris and New York Bars, he practised international business law, has wide experience in international transactions and transnational disputes, and has been acting as an arbitrator since the 1980s in the EU and the US. A co-chair of the ICC Task Force on Arbitration of Climate Change-related Disputes, he co-edited the ICC Institute of World Business Law's XXIst Dossier on Navigating the New Contents of International Public Policy: Compliance in Environment and Human Rights. Patrick Thieffry has been teaching environmental law since 1996 at the Sorbonne as an associate professor between 2008 and 2019 and in several other universities, including Paris 2 Panthéon-Assas on arbitration of environment and climate disputes. He authored a *Handbook of European Environmental and Climate Law* (Bruylant, 2nd ed. 2021), a *Traité de droit européen de l'environnement et du climat* (Bruylant, 4th ed. 2020,), a *Manuel de droit européen de l'environnement et du climat* (Bruylant, 3rd ed., 2021) as well as other books and many articles on international arbitration, business, and environmental law. He holds degrees in International Economics and International Private Law, practised in the US for five years and presented a PhD thesis on Environmental Law.

# Summary of Contents

# Table of Contents

# Foreword

Few topics for an arbitration conference are not only more topical but also more unsettling than the impact of ESG – disputes involving environmental, social or governance issues. It is topical because ESG covers relatively new international challenges that require new approaches to dispute resolution. We, the arbitration community, need answers, and we need to provide them ourselves. The 2023 ASA conference on 'ESG and disputes: flash in the pan or game changer?' discussed the challenges and developed some answers. The discussion will continue. The topic is also unsettling because it shines an awkward spotlight on one of the darker corners of international arbitration: the ever-increasing carbon footprint of our typical arbitration practices.

The conference was timely and a great success, thanks to the careful and thoughtful organization by James Menz and Urs Weber-Stecher and the excellent moderators and panellists with diverse backgrounds. This book contains the contributions of many speakers and has been carefully edited by James and Urs. It is a testament to their pioneering work and will hopefully serve as a welcome basis for further discussion within the global arbitration community on ESG disputes.

*Felix Dasser*
*ASA President*
*Zurich, June 2024*

# Introduction

*Urs Weber-Stecher & James Menz*

The question posed in the title of the conference can be answered clearly after the conference: ESG is not just a flash in the pan for disputes, neither for commercial nor for investment disputes!

The latest developments show that ESG and disputes were not only a 'hot button' in February 2023, when the conference took place, but will remain so for the foreseeable future. We recently saw in all media channels that the *Climate Women Seniors* won their ECHR litigation against Switzerland – a historic judgment that has received mixed commentary – and the European Union passed a supply chain act, requiring large companies to conduct human rights and environmental due diligence in their own operations and in their global value chains.

The conference was divided into four parts to cover the different angles in which ESG manifests itself in international disputes: (1) an overview to clarify terminology and the general trends; (2) commercial dispute resolution; (3) investment dispute resolution; and (4) the practice of arbitration today. Consistent with ASA's user focus, we ensured the presence of in-house or governmental representatives on each panel. We also benefited from the third co-chair of the conference, Annette Magnusson, Climate Change Counsel and former Secretary General of SCC, who shared her insights into the topic and network of contacts.

All panellists identified sources of litigation and arbitration, some from perhaps somewhat unexpected corners. If only a fraction of these trends bear out, we should see a notable increase in demand for the service of ESG-literate arbitrators and counsel.

Panel 1: The ESG Disputes Landscape Today: Challenges and Responses. In Chapter 1 on nature capital, nature markets and arbitration, *Crenguta Leaua* and *Leonardo Conte* trace the origin of ESG to two fundamental trends: (i) attaching a monetary value to the protection of nature, and (ii) attaching nature-protection-related values to money. Broadly, nature-related assets and markets dealing in nature-related products have emerged. They describe an 'explosion' of human rights and environment-related disputes, e.g., climate change litigation, as one metric of this trend, with over 2,000 cases having been registered so far. They also predict an increase in arbitrations in the 'nature markets' identified in the article and certain particular trends, such as more objections on arbitrability, participation of non-signatories, and the interrelationship with state court litigations.

In Chapter 2 on ESG and international arbitration: general considerations, *Patrick Thieffry* discusses the growth of ESG due to policy developments, forecasts an increase in ESG arbitrations as the number and depth of regulations increases, and posits that enhanced transparency in arbitration might be necessary to make arbitration more socially acceptable to stakeholders.

Panel 2: Commercial dispute resolution: ESG Ante Portas? In Chapter 3 on arbitration as a means for resolving climate change-related disputes, *Moritz Keller* and *Sunny Kapoor* address the taxonomy of direct climate change disputes (e.g., the Shell litigation, Indonesian fishermen against Holcim) – litigation, and typical issues, and 'indirect' climate change and ESG disputes a good portion of which will go to arbitration. They identify which disputes could trigger which type of arbitrations (e.g., energy transition disputes, ESG-compliant supply chain).

In Chapter 4, Isabelle Romy contributes to the board of directors' perspective. She emphasizes that nowadays, ESG has everyone's attention on the board. She notes that courts (and arbitral tribunals?) are becoming vehicles for effecting policy changes and going beyond compliance with mandatory law. She identifies reporting and D&O liability as a possible source of disputes and arbitration clauses in the articles of incorporation as a potential risk mitigation measure (arbitration's advantages could become useful to help blunt the effort to turn public courts into pressure tools).

Panel 3: ESG in Investment Arbitration: Status and Trends. In Chapter 5 on the Energy Charter Treaty and its role in the energy transition, *Samantha J. Rowe* shares the investment law perspective and discusses the ECT withdrawal by European states and how the ECT has come to be perceived to block the green transition – and she responds to this criticism. She further sketches out the future of the ECT and potential changes and modernization to help it become part of the 'solution', i.e., a tool to support the energy transition. In her view, the ECT remains highly relevant, not least because of the sunset clause protecting existing investments twenty years after the termination of the treaty.

In Chapter 6, Discussion on the Environmental Footprint of Arbitration Practitioners: Towards Greener Arbitrations?, *Urs Weber-Stecher* summarizes the panel discussion on the environmental footprint of arbitration practitioners. The panellists addressed the personal responsibility of everyone involved in arbitration from different angles: from the perspective of the arbitrator, the arbitral institution, the external counsel representing companies in arbitration proceedings and, most importantly, the in-house counsel as the user of arbitration services. The discussion focussed on very concrete ways in which each and every arbitration practitioner can contribute to a more environmentally friendly and socially responsible arbitration practice.

# PANEL 1 The ESG Disputes Landscape Today: Challenges and Responses

# CHAPTER 1
# Nature Capital, Nature Markets and Arbitration

*Crenguta Leaua & Leonardo Conte*

## §1.01 INTRODUCTION

In the legal world, originated in ethics, we speak the 'language' of rights and obligations, and of their underlying values. All laws, contracts, and all procedural documents in dispute resolution and all enforcements afterwards refer to rights, obligations, values, and principles.

In the business world, originated in economics, one speaks the 'language' of capital, and its monetary value. In the business environment, all the financial situations, all the reports, and all the purposes that are expressed at some point in time by a corporation are ultimately referred to in monetary terms as the sole measurement of capital. Here, even non-monetary values would be considered in these terms, and one can speak about human capital, natural capital, and others.

Values and money are therefore the keywords when it comes to identifying what is causing a legal dispute in the business world: a clash in values and/or a clash in monetary interests. If we were to refer to nature protection, looking at the fundamental cause of environmental protection disputes, the most interesting part is the relationship between the relevant values (i.e., protection of the environment, respect for human life) and money. To prevent and solve these disputes, one may wish to build a common denominator or at least a fair translation between the language of values and that of money.

For the legal world, the translation is rather familiar, as frequently, the values (incorporated in rights and obligations) are expressed in monetary terms. Indeed, lawyers are using experts in valuation to make precisely this translation by measuring the impact of various actions on the values to reach the monetary compensation in case of those values being damaged (i.e., liability and tort), or perhaps split profits in case of agreements to share benefits (i.e., joint ventures, partnerships), or define the monetary rights in terms of risk management (i.e., various insurances where compensation needs to be quantified).

For the business environment, the reverse translation, from money to values, is not such a familiar operation, though some concepts enable such translation. For instance, Corporate Social Responsibility (CSR) measures are being implemented by companies and have become an integral part of corporations' financial situation.

However, a more direct connection between money and values is currently developing at the international level, and such connection can be seen in the field of nature protection with regard to two recent trends. These are indeed advancing the relationship between money and values from a simple translation exercise to actual interconnectivity, profoundly linking the climate protection values with the monetary aspects in the life of both corporations and states.

A first trend is *attaching a monetary value to the respect of the nature protection-related values*; this is the creation of the notion of value-capital, a new concept that includes that of nature as capital. We shall refer in detail to the concept and its implications in the following parts of this chapter.

A second trend, the very opposite of the first, is *attaching nature protection-related values to the money*; this is the creation of a nature protection-related scoring system to be used in the financial sector for controlling money use with respect to the desired values. Basically, the circuit of money is restricted based on the respect of a value.

If we were to think in terms of an analogy, since money can be considered the 'blood' of an economy, attaching ethical values to it would ensure the efficient distribution and observance of those values throughout the social organism. This is in fact not a completely new concept, as, for instance, at the fall of communism, the Eastern European countries receiving financing from various international organizations (e.g., International Monetary Fund or European Bank for Reconstruction and Development) had to comply with certain social parameters related with the observance of values such as democracy, rule of law, and anti-corruption.

For nature protection, the concept was launched in 2022 under the name of Swiss Climate Scores,[1] with the aim to allow the financing only of those projects which are compliant with the scores reflecting the technical requirements as provided by COP 21 for environmental protection purposes. The Federal Council instructed the Federal Department of Finance to work in cooperation with the Federal Department of Environment, Transport, Energy and Communications in order to investigate the voluntary uptake at the moment of the launch of the project, with the aim to be generalized in the Swiss financial market by the end of 2023.

Similarly, the EU is regulating environmental, social, and corporate governance (ESG) scoring and rating activities in order to increase transparency for financial

1. *See* Swiss Climate Scores, https://www.sif.admin.ch/sif/en/home/swiss-climate-scores/brief-summary.html.

investors.[2] In this spirit, the OECD is also providing guidance and policy recommendations for governments willing to foster ESG investing.[3] Despite its methodological issues and critics, ESG scoring can not only foster the climate transition but also create economic value for the companies and markets choosing to embrace them.[4]

In this context, once the value-money or the money-value becomes part of our language in both law and economics, we can see how nature markets are developed and how contracts are formed between the participants in these markets. The aim of this chapter is to explore this phenomenon to then refer to the potential role of arbitration in solving the disputes specific to these markets.

## §1.02 NATURE PROTECTION AS CAPITAL

### [A] The Conceptualization of Nature as Capital

As mentioned, economics is not a stranger to the concept of value, except that it typically frames *value* as *capital* and thus quantifies it in *money*. It conceptualizes values as linked to resources, and hence, it refers to human capital, social capital, cultural capital, natural capital, and so on from the perspective of being (economic) resources. Despite all the limits that this approach entails and the impacts on policy and business decision-making that these limitations necessarily have[5], it is arguably the case that most human society-related phenomena are very complex and thus difficult to measure in quantitative – or monetary – terms. Among them, nature, natural elements, and environmental factors are some of the hardest to evaluate and assess economically.

Nevertheless, attempts to do so have been increasingly done in the last two decades. One that is having major success is called 'ecosystem services valuation' and

2. European Parliament, 'Environmental, Social and Governance (ESG) rating activities: Commission proposal for a Regulation on their transparency and integrity', 15 December 2023, https://www.europarl.europa.eu/legislative-train/theme-an-economy-that-works-for-people/file-esg-rating#: ~ :text = Environmental%2C%20Social%20and%20Governance%20(ESG)%20rating%20activities%20play%20an,risk%20management%20on%20ESG%20factors; *see also* ESMA Report on Trends, Risks and Vulnerabilities, 2021, https://www.esma.europa.eu/sites/default/files/trv_2021_1-esg_ratings_status_and_key_issues_ahead.pdf.
3. OECD, 'Policy guidance on market practices to strengthen ESG investing and finance a climate transition', 2022, https://www.oecd-ilibrary.org/docserver/2c5b535c-en.pdf?expires = 1705489489&id = id&accname = guest&checksum = 2E76C74CD7759F98E9CB995104A5C534.
4. *See* McKinsey, 'Five Ways That ESG Creates Value', November 2021, https://www.mckinsey.com/ ~ /media/McKinsey/Business%20Functions/Strategy%20and%20Corporate%20Finance/Our%20Insights/Five%20ways%20that%20ESG%20creates%20value/Five-ways-that-ESG-creates-value.ashx.
5. C.L. Spash and V. Asara, 'Ecological Economics: From Nature to Society', in L. Fischer, J. Hasell, J.C. Proctor, D. Uwakwe, Z. Ward-Perkins and C. Watson, *Rethinking Economics: An Introduction to Pluralist Economics*, 2018, London: Routledge; A. Buller, 'The Value of a Whale: On the Illusions of Green Capitalism', 2022, Manchester: Manchester University Press.

pursues the quantification – in monetary terms – of the 'services' that nature provides.[6] In particular, it measures the value of the natural elements by assessing the potential costs of not disposing of clean water, breathable air, and other crucial factors determining human survival on Earth. As explained by an official release of the US White House:

> Because nature provides us with so many things without cost, these benefits – called 'ecosystem services' – are not always fully captured in benefit-cost analysis. [...] Failing to fully account for nature's bounty has led to under-valuing and erosion of our nation's natural assets. [...] We must measure what we value, not just value what is simple to measure.[7]

Besides relevant risks of commodification[8] and fundamental issues of social justice,[9] accounting for ecosystem services in traditional cost-benefit analysis (CBA) can reveal, in numbers (e.g., dollars), the importance of these natural elements both for our society and the economy.

Drawing upon this rationale, the Capitals Coalition conceives *nature* and natural elements as *capital*, namely a resource storing and providing economic value to owners and exchangers.[10] Whereas the value of nature has not been embedded in economic transactions whatsoever, the concept of 'natural capital' gives organizations the possibility to create economic value for nature by investing in it. In order to do so, the so-called Natural Capital Protocol (NCP) built 'a decision-making framework that enables organizations to identify, measure and value their direct and indirect impacts and dependencies on natural capital'.[11]

Once those natural elements are capitalized, one can invest in them. The so-called investments in conservation allow conserving natural environments by attracting foreign capital investments for protecting natural reserves.[12] In so doing, investors create value through the protection of natural resources, and investments become a way to leverage the natural environment to preserve existing natural spaces.

---

6. M. Sagoff, 'The Quantification and Valuation of Ecosystem Services', *Ecological Economics*, 70(3), pp. 497-502, 2011 DOI: 10.1016/j.ecolecon.2010.10.006; Y.E. Chee, 'An Ecological Perspective on the Valuation of Ecosystem Services', *Biological Conservation*, 120(4), pp. 549-565, 2014 DOI: 10.1016/j.biocon.2004.03.028.
7. The White House, 'Accounting for Ecosystem Services in Benefit-Cost Analysis', 2023, 1 August, https://www.whitehouse.gov/omb/briefing-room/2023/08/01/accounting-for-ecosystem-services-in-benefit-cost-analysis/.
8. E. Gómez-Baggethun and M. Ruiz-Pérez, 'Economic Valuation and the Commodification of Ecosystem Services', *Progress in Physical Geography: Earth and Environment*, 35(5), 2011, pp. 613-628 DOI: 10.1177/0309133311421708; J. Smessaert, A. Missemer and H. Levrel, 'The Commodification of Nature: A Review in Social Sciences', *Ecological Economics*, 172, 2020 DOI: 10.1016/j.ecolecon.2020.106624.
9. B.S. Matulis, 'The Economic Valuation of Nature: A Question of Justice?', *Ecological Economics*, 104, pp. 155-157, 2014 DOI: 10.1016/j.ecolecon.2014.04.010; E. Corbera, 'Valuing Nature, Paying for Ecosystem Services and Realizing Social Justice: A Response to Matulis (2014)', *Ecological Economics*, 110, pp. 154-157, 2015 DOI: 10.1016/j.ecolecon.2014.12.017.
10. Capitals Coalition, https://capitalscoalition.org/capitals-approach/natural-capital-protocol/?fwp_filter_tabs=guide_supplement.
11. *Ibid.*
12. Invest Conservation, https://investconservation.com/; Recelio, https://recelio.org/.

For instance, through biodiversity ESG reporting, investors 'in nature' can capitalize their investments and local owners thus become obliged to preserve their areas' biodiversity. Natural resources are then seen as potential sources of new – previously 'hidden' – economic value, and *value in conservation* emerges.[13]

### [B] The Nature-Related Assets

Whereas 'nature has mostly been seen as an infinite property to be extracted rather than a regenerative life source to be protected',[14] the rising awareness of climate change and increasing environmental concerns are leading the active conservation of natural elements to ultimately become more valuable; also financially. As a result, 'pricing nature across the global economy could increase the potential for nature to be preserved, invested in, and restored'.[15] That is, new sources of value are created by preserving existing natural elements.

Considering the existing natural elements as resources to be preserved rather than raw materials to be exploited ultimately makes natural capital an *asset*. Here, existing natural resources are preserved and ultimately valued more through their protection. In this sense, there is *value in the conservation* of these natural resources.[16]

There are various types of nature assets that can be already found in the economy:

- nature-related assets referring to the ownership of the rights to exploit the natural resources themselves (e.g., land rights, fresh-water rights) or a full ecosystem (e.g., forest, island);
- natural products seen as commodities (e.g., wood, natural fruits, wild species);
- nature-related credits, such as carbon credits,[17] biodiversity credits,[18] etc.;
- financial rights tied to the assets, products, commodities or credits (e.g., commodity derivatives,[19] nature-related insurance[20]).[21]

---

13. *Ibid.*
14. Taskforce on Nature Markets, 'The Rights of Nature: Developments and Implications for the Governance of Nature Markets', 2022, p. 20.
15. Taskforce on Nature Markets, 'Making Nature Markets Work: Shaping a Global Nature Economy in the 21st Century', 2023, p. 20.
16. For a discussion, *see* LombardOdier, 'Revaluing Nature – The World's Most Under-priced Asset Class', 2023, https://www.lombardodier.com/contents/corporate-news/corporate/2023/september/revaluing-nature-the-world's-mos.html; *see also* Taskforce on Nature-related Financial Disclosure, 'Why nature matters', https://tnfd.global/about/why-nature-matters/.
17. For example, *see* Verra, 'Verified Carbon Standard', https://verra.org/programs/verified-carbon-standard/.
18. For example, *see* The Biodiversity Consultancy, 'Biodiversity Credits', https://www.thebiodiversityconsultancy.com/our-work/what-we-do/for-companies/biodiversity-credits/.
19. For an overview, *see* N.C. Schofield, *Commodity Derivatives: Markets and Applications*, Wiley, 2021.
20. For examples, *see* SwissRe, 'Insurance to protect and enable nature-based solutions', https://www.swissre.com/our-business/public-sector-solutions/insurance-to-protect-and-enable-nature-based-solutions.html; Zurich, 'Nature and biodiversity', https://www.zurich.com/en/sustainability/planet/nature-and-biodiversity.

In the current technical development, many of these rights may also be found in digital support by way of tokenization (the nature-rights non-fungible tokens (NFTs)).[22]

These financial systems are created ad hoc in order to make investments in nature more efficient, ultimately fostering environmental protection through the creation of marketplaces and wallets dedicated to nature-related assets. Indeed, these could be finally inserted into ESG reporting and thus bound investors to capitalize on nature and owners to preserve their natural resources.

### [C] The Nature Markets

Once that transactions are possible with nature-related assets, markets emerge. In the context of this chapter, we refer to a 'market' intended as the meeting of supply and demand for certain goods. The market can be physical or virtual. For instance, it could be a platform (e.g., marketplace, exchange) – more or less organized and formalized – where these goods are exchanged and traded. 'Nature markets' can be defined as those markets arising whenever 'an explicit economic value of nature is identified and can be traded'.[23]

These include credit markets, asset markets, intrinsic markets, and derivative markets,[24] each of them having different 'products' being exchanged:

- asset markets, where the traded object is the rights to use specific natural assets (e.g., water trading markets[25]);
- commodity markets, built out of the exchange of natural commodities (e.g., New York Mercantile Exchange, London Metal Exchange);
- credit markets, where carbon credits or biodiversity credits are traded (e.g., Carbon Trade Exchange, Ecosystem Marketplace);[26]
- derivative markets, where the financial products tied to natural assets, commodities or credits are traded.[27]

---

21. For the distinction, *see* Taskforce on Nature Markets, https://www.naturemarkets.net/.
22. *See*, for instance, KlimaDAO, https://docs.klimadao.finance/; Moss Amazon NFT, https://nft.moss.earth/.
23. Taskforce on Nature Markets, 'Making Nature Markets Work: Shaping a Global Nature Economy in the 21st Century', 2023, p. 18.
24. *Ibid.*, p. 19; *see also* McKinsey, 'The State of Nature Markets Today and Tomorrow', 9 December 2022, https://www.mckinsey.com/capabilities/sustainability/our-insights/sustainability-blog/the-state-of-nature-markets-today-and-tomorrow.
25. For an overview, *see* C. Lai, 'Water Trading Market: A Solution to Water Scarcity?', 21 February 2023, https://earth.org/water-trading-market/.
26. For an overview, *see* Taskforce on Nature Markets, 'Biodiversity Credit Markets: The role of law, regulation and policy', 2023, April, https://www.naturemarkets.net/publications/biodiversity-credit-markets.
27. For an overview, *see* FIA, 'How derivatives markets are helping the world fight climate change', September 2020, https://www.fia.org/sites/default/files/2020-08/FIA%20Climate%20Change%20Policy%20Paper_0.pdf.

As a development of the last few years, in the situation of tokenized nature rights, digital marketplaces have developed.[28]

Instead of a 'one-size-fits-all' solution, the Taskforce on Nature Markets[29] – which is responsible for fostering, establishing, and governing nature markets – warns that:

> The rise of nature markets does not automatically guarantee better outcomes. Indeed, left simply to evolve in their own way they could even make things worse.[30]

For this reason, in order to 'make nature markets work' and reach positive outcomes, the Taskforce suggests not exclusively focusing on market-based solutions but rather complementing that through 'political and policy actions needed to transform the basis on which enterprises, markets and economies use, invest in, trade, and pay for nature'.[31]

Indeed, the infrastructure of nature markets shall be reinforced by consumers' and citizens' voices, choices, and investment decisions and supported by governments and regulators through fiscal and regulatory acts.[32] As noted by the Taskforce:

> In some instances, the key may be to advance greater transparency, amplify stakeholder voices, or improve price discovery and liquidity. In other instances, regulatory developments may be the essential piece – whether judicial action, deploying innovative legal instruments, financial regulations or setting new standards.[33]

This shall be further supported by 'policy incentives, regulation, and new governance frameworks at the local, regional, and international levels'.[34]

## §1.03 DISPUTES IN NATURE MARKETS

### [A] Participants of Nature Markets

Different actors and stakeholders are engaged with nature markets. First, the companies: (1) interested in (or obliged to) buying nature-related credits (e.g., carbon credits) or ecosystem assets (e.g., water rights) in order to operate (or compensate for) their business activities; (2) owning the commodities, ecosystem services, or right to access

28. *See*, for instance, Toucan, https://toucan.earth/; for a general concept of a decentralized marketplace for nature-based solutions *see* Cambridge Centre for Carbon Credits (4C), https://4c.cst.cam.ac.uk/about/marketplace.
29. Taskforce on Nature Markets, https://www.naturemarkets.net/.
30. Taskforce on Nature Markets, 'Making Nature Markets Work: Shaping a Global Nature Economy in the 21st Century', 2023, p. 2.
31. *Ibid.*, p. 41.
32. *Ibid.*, p. 20; *see*, for instance, the Australia's Nature Repair Bill and the UK's Nature Market Regulatory Framework.
33. Taskforce on Nature Markets, 'Making Nature Markets Work: Shaping a Global Nature Economy in the 21st Century', 2023, p. 39.
34. *Ibid.*, p. 41.

the natural resources traded (e.g., wildlife tourism); and (3) trading (i.e., acting as intermediaries for) nature-related assets, rights, ecosystem services, and financial products directly tied to these products (e.g., biodiversity loss insurance, water futures).

Second, the states, regulators, and entities provisioning, regulating, and releasing the rights to use natural resources and the natural assets themselves. Since these have the direct power to preserve their natural spaces, they represent the ultimate responsible actor for natural protection. Here, 'nature rich countries' of the Global South aim at gaining comparative advantages in natural elements' trade by monetizing them faster and wider. Instead, 'economically wealthier countries' seek to preserve natural elements for the sake of climate change, trying to maximize their food security and value chain benefits and minimize their monetary costs, for instance, by adopting new technologies for the ecological transition (i.e., de-coupling, circularity).[35]

Third, the natural elements themselves represent a key, new actor in nature markets. This way, these are treated *as if* they were humans having citizen rights. The so-called rights of nature give voice to natural elements, in both markets and legal settings. As explained by the Taskforce on Nature Markets:

> Rights of Nature (RoN) encompasses a range of legal mechanisms giving nature a right to have its interests be argued before the law and found in favour of by courts, as though it were a human litigant. [It] is a term encompassing two related things: (1) a legal philosophy, and (2) legal provisions that codify this philosophy by recognizing ecosystems as subjects with rights.[36]

Adopted in order to further protect nature's right to exist, continue existing, and be restored, this legal concept complements the economic one of ecosystem services (*see* above). On top of market-type incentives, this approach provides effective frameworks to incentivize the protection of nature and penalize its active degradation.[37]

In fact, countries have been providing legal personhood to their natural resources and giving legal status to their territories' natural elements, such as forests and rivers. For instance, Ecuador constitutionally recognized the rights of natural elements and applied them in the case of the Los Cedros Forest in 2021. Similarly, the New Zealand Parliament approved acts that provide legal personhood to a national park and a river, and India did the same with its Ganga and Yamuna rivers.[38] More recently, the rights

35. *Ibid.*, pp. 25-26.
36. Taskforce on Nature Markets, 'The Rights of Nature: Developments and Implications for the Governance of Nature Markets', 2022, p. 9.
37. *Ibid.*, p. 18.
38. 'The Urewera Act, Legal identity of Te Urewera and vesting of Te Urewera land', New Zealand Government, 2014, https://www.legislation.govt.nz/act/public/2014/0051/latest/DLM6183705.html; 'Te Awa Tupua Act (Whanganui River Claims Settlement)', New Zealand Government, 2017, https://www.legislation.govt.nz/act/public/2017/0007/latest/whole.html; S. Sharma, 'Ganga and Yamuna as a Living Entity: What Does This Mean to the Rivers?', 2017, https://legalserviceindia.com/legal/article-8146-ganga-and-yamuna-as-a-living-entity-what-does-this-mean-to-the-rivers-.html#:~:text=What%20Does%20This%20Title%20Mean,considered%20as%20the%20legal%20person.

of Lake Erie Bill and Grant Township were recognized by the US Federal Court and the Pennsylvania State Court, respectively.[39]

Fourth, civil society becomes a key factor in nature markets. Not only environmental defenders, climate and human rights activists, and structured non-governmental organizations (NGOs) but also single citizens and consumers have the right to sue governments and organizations deemed responsible for any type of environmental degradation. Together with the local communities directly and most harshly affected by its destructive effects (e.g., indigenous people), citizens from the Global North – indirectly hit by the effects and subject to the costs of climate change – gain the voice and political power to effectively influence nature markets.[40] In fact:

> Many natural entities are not merely confined to national borders, and the actions of those across a border can greatly affect the health of a natural entity elsewhere [...] These solutions come in the shape of norms and principles once siloed off from environmental law but now being given new life in innovative ways and used and endorsed by a plethora of actors, from states to corporations to individual citizens, all with the express aim of securing a thriving and healthy environment.[41]

Although the rights of nature clearly bring potential legal consequences for those afflicting any 'offence' to the former, it also further complicates the legal procedures to ensure their effective application, thus calling for a legal apparatus supporting rising conflicts over natural elements.

### [B] The Context of the Disputes in Nature Markets

Disputes in nature markets have to be seen from a dual perspective: on the one hand, as contractual disputes between the parties to the specific transactions and, on the other hand, as part of a broader picture of disputes in the field of environmental protection. This second element is important as it generates a particularly litigious market.

Disputes in the field of environmental protection may arise from different legal provisions, human rights being the most visible one. With international organizations recognizing the human rights to a healthy environment and some countries introducing it constitutionally or through regional treaties, the criminal act of 'ecocide' and all practices damaging natural elements are becoming arrestable offences,[42] extending

39. Taskforce on Nature Markets, 'The Rights of Nature: Developments and implications for the governance of nature markets', 2022, pp. 10-11.
40. Taskforce on Nature Markets, 'Making Nature Markets Work: Shaping a Global Nature Economy in the 21st Century', 2023, pp. 39-41.
41. Taskforce on Nature Markets, 'The Rights of Nature: Developments and Implications for the Governance of Nature Markets', 2022, pp. 19-20.
42. Regional treaties include the Aarhus Convention and the ECLAC Agreement, and the United Nations Economic Commission for Europe Convention on Access to Information, Public Participation in Decision-Making and Access to Justice in Environmental Matters (Aarhus) in 1998. International organizations include the United Nations Human Rights Council and the United Nations General Assembly.

liability to whoever is 'responsible for acts and decisions that lead to severe environmental harm' thus making them prosecutable.[43] As a consequence, recent years have seen, not surprisingly:

> An explosion in cases concerning the intersection between environmental and human rights law [...] Using both substantive and procedural rights, the shape, scope, and obligations of a right to a healthy environment have been teased out by judiciaries worldwide.[44]

Moreover, 'climate change litigation is increasing and broadening in geographical reach, while the range of legal theories is expanding'[45] (*see* Figure 1.1). In particular, 2,000 + cases of climate change litigation have so far been registered (1,500 only in the United States) in 60 + jurisdictions and international or regional courts, as well as other judicial bodies (*see* Figure 1.2).

*Figure 1.1 Cumulative Percentage of Cases According to Geographical Representation (Cases in the Global South Versus Cases in the Global North Excluding the United States of America Through 31 December 2022)*

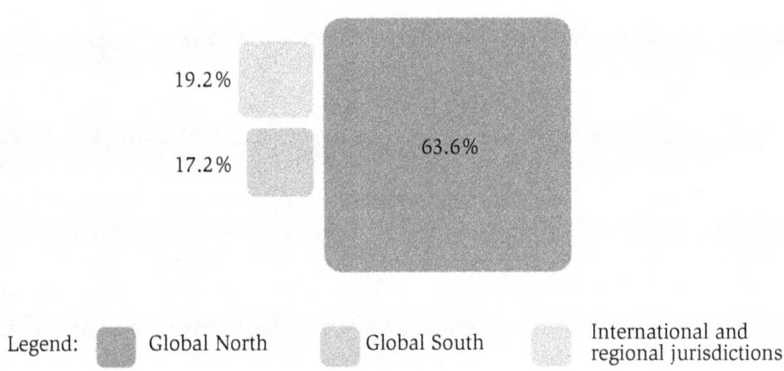


*Source*: Global Climate Litigation Report: 2023 Status Review.

43. Taskforce on Nature Markets, 'The Rights of Nature: Developments and Implications for the Governance of Nature Markets', 2022, p. 8.
44. *Ibid.*, pp. 5-6.
45. 'Global Climate Litigation Report: 2023 Status Review', United Nations Environment Programme, 2023, Nairobi, p. XIV.

*Figure 1.2 Growth of Climate Change Litigation (as Represented in the 2017, 2020 and 2023 Litigation Reports)*

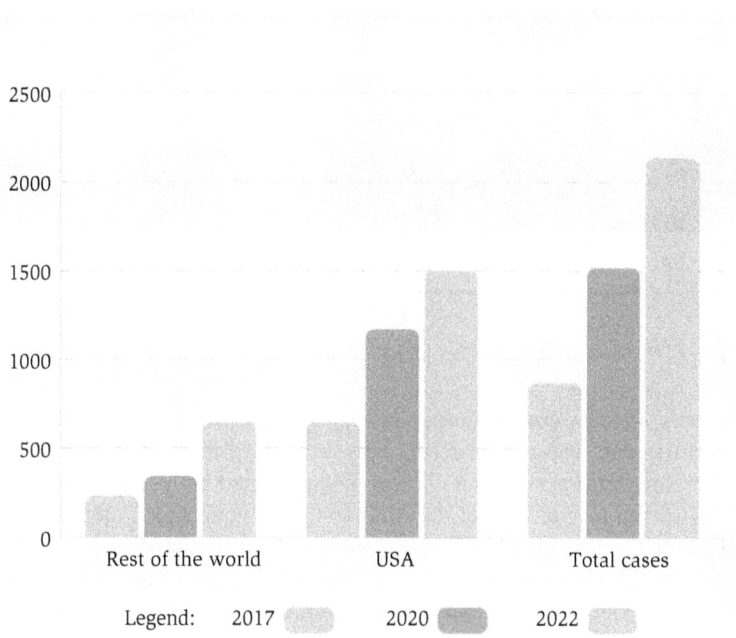


*Source*: Global Climate Litigation Report: 2023 Status Review.

Climate litigation cases typically include the use of climate rights, the domestic enforcement of international commitments, corporate liability (i.e., duty for mitigating emissions or adapting to climate change), and climate disclosures (i.e., protection of investors and consumers).[46] That is, actors usually ask for the enforcement of climate laws, the integration of climate action into existing laws, the establishment of obligations for those responsible for environmental degradation, and compensation for climate harms.[47] Indeed, most have been addressed against corporate actors (e.g., Carbon Majors) with a complex range of legal arguments, and 50% of them have direct judicial outcomes as favourable to climate action (*see* Figure 1.3).[48]

46. *See ibid.*, Part 3, pp. 26-60.
47. *Ibid.*, p. XI; for issues of compensation, *see* 'Climate-Related Financial Risk Factors in Compensation Frameworks', Financial Stability Board, 2023, 20 April, https://www.fsb.org/wp-content/uploads/P204023.pdf.
48. J. Setzer & C. Higham, 'Global Trends in Climate Change Litigation: 2023 Snapshot', London: LSE, 2023; *see also* 'Global Climate Litigation Report: 2023 Status Review', United Nations Environment Programme, 2023, Nairobi.

*Figure 1.3 The Shapshot from the Report with the Whole Content*

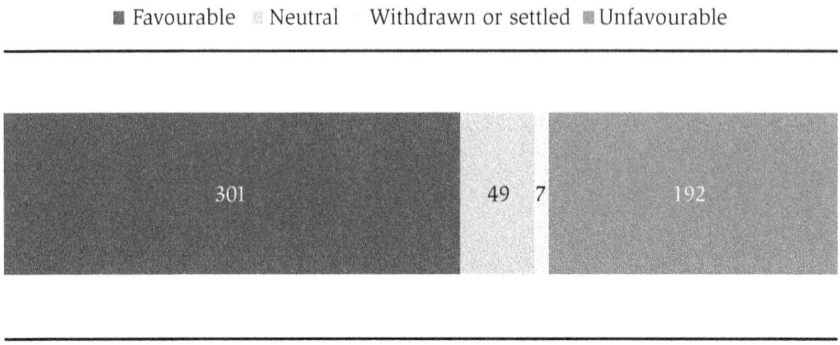


*Source*: Global Trends in Climate Change Litigation: 2023 Snapshot.

Not only are new parties given the capacity to file a claim (*see* above) but also new procedures and responsible actors arise, with surprising outcomes. For instance, the US Supreme Court set off that climate disputes shall be heard by Federal or State Courts,[49] with the recent case of the Montana state government standing out;[50] the Nepal Supreme Court extended the realm of ecocide to the excavation of stone, gravel, and sand;[51] the Düsseldorf Regional Court proceeded against Total's claims to climate neutrality of its heating oil;[52] and fossil fuel companies' directors and financiers became directly liable for environmental degradation.[53]

49. The Guardian, 'US Supreme Court Denies Oil Companies' Bid to Move Venue of Climate Lawsuits', 24 April 2023, https://www.theguardian.com/law/2023/apr/24/supreme-court-oil-climate-lawsuits-state-federal#: ~ :text = The%20US%20supreme%20court%20on,Energy%20 Inc%20and%20Chevron%20Corp.
50. The Guardian, '"Gamechanger": Judge Rules in Favor of Young Activists in US Climate Trial', 14 August 2023, https://amp-theguardian-com.cdn.ampproject.org/c/s/amp.theguardian.com/us-news/2023/aug/14/montana-climate-trial-young-activists-judge-order; *see* the victory order here: https://westernlaw.org/wp-content/uploads/2023/08/2023.08.14-Held-v.-Montana-victory-order.pdf.
51. Nepal Supreme Court, 'Shailendra Prasad Ambedkar v. Office of Prime Minister et. al.', 2021, http://climatecasechart.com/non-us-case/shailendra-prasad-ambedkar-v-office-of-prime-minister-et-al/.
52. Deutsche Umwelthilfe, 'Verbrauchertäuschung mit vermeintlicher "Klimaneutralität": Deutsche Umwelthilfe gewinnt vor Gericht gegen TotalEnergies wegen angeblich "CO2-kompensiertem Heizöl"', 5 April 2023, https://www.presseportal.de/pm/22521/5480104.
53. 'Okpabi v. Shell Appeal Highlights Important Points Regarding Parent Company Liability', Simmons & Simmons, 26 February 2018, https://www.simmons-simmons.com/en/publications/ck0aui07qnmjj0b850lndx43e/260218-okpabi-v-shell. *See also* UN letter to Aramco: https://spcommreports.ohchr.org/TMResultsBase/DownLoadPublicCommunicationFile?gId = 28094.

### [C] Arbitration for Nature Markets-Related Disputes

International arbitration is the most suitable fora for the nature markets-related disputes for a number of reasons, the most obvious one being:

- the adaptability of arbitration to novel business and technical areas, such as the new nature rights or their tokenization;
- possibility to decide the cases *ex aequo et bono* or using *amiable compositeur*, particularly useful in areas where the legislation is too novel or the opposite is outdated;
- the possibility to appoint arbitrators with relevant scientific or environmental knowledge or with the required economic background to address the specificity of the nature markets;
- availability of a broader range of technical experts and in general more flexible evidentiary rules;
- the confidentiality, potentially important for certain information about natural resources;
- the neutrality of arbitration in case parties have concerns about the local courts in certain jurisdictions; and
- the international enforceability that may be needed in case of international business relationships.

When looking at the use of commercial arbitration for nature market disputes in the current context of the development of international policy, legislation and litigation, one can identify some potential trends to be considered.

#### *[1] Increase of the Objections on Arbitrability*

As long as the assets, commodities or derivatives are legally traded, normally disputes arising out or in connection with the traded rights are likely to be arbitrable. However, the situation may no longer be as simple if the dispute falls into the category of situations where national legislation may provide the local courts with exclusive jurisdiction on specific types of assets or for specific types of contracts. Natural resources may be falling in such a category, and so public contracts referring to them (concession agreements, PPPs, etc.).

#### *[2] Increased Pressure for the Participation of Non-signatories*

Participation of non-signatories is likely to be a developing trend in the context in which the protection of nature is capturing the public interest. It is to be expected that tribunals in commercial arbitration will face requests for *amicus curiae,* similar to those in investment arbitration, or even more intrusive requests, such as request for joinder, from not only environmental NGOs but also concerned citizens.

### [3] *Relationship with Other Pending Litigations of Relevance to the Subject of the Dispute*

Due to the vast range of possible fora where disputes related to the protection of nature may be brought, as well as the wide range of potential claimants, there are two main issues likely to raise specific challenges for the commercial arbitration originating in the transactions with nature-related rights: (i) the issue of the pending disputes addressing the same factual situation from different legal perspectives, and (ii) the issue of the correlation and sequence between the outcome of such cases.

### [4] *A Certain Migration from Investment Towards Commercial Arbitration*

In the field of investment arbitration, the social movements regarding nature protection in the context of climate change and the international policy in the field of ESG clearly point to a future in which states are to develop various interventionist measures to address the protection of nature. That means that the topic of nature protection is likely to be the most active one with reference to the regulatory space in investment protection treaties. While most bilateral investment treaties (BITs) renegotiations produce treaties with less room for host governments to regulate, some states initiated efforts to renegotiate their BITs, as far as ISDS is concerned, for the purpose of preserving more of their regulatory space. In the foreseeable future situation, some of the disputes that would have been previously referred to investment arbitration may fall out of the scope of the treaty protection and therefore investors may be 'pushed' to try to address the issues of the change in legislation affecting their nature-related rights in the context of contractual disputes under their contracts with the relevant state entities. That would lead to investors being inclined to insist more on having arbitration agreements inserted in the contracts they enter with state entities and also for commercial arbitration cases being more frequently used in cases in which parties would have preferred the path of investment arbitration.

Additionally, the pressure of civil society at national and international levels is calling on the states to enable various mechanisms for ensuring state compliance with its international environmental obligation. Governmental contracts may be requested to include specific provisions in which parties are bound to respect both domestic and international obligations in the field of environmental law. This is already seen in practice and may lead to a situation in which a breach of the provisions of international treaties in the field of environmental protection (or, more broader, the ESG) may be defined as a contractual breach as well. In such cases, the commercial arbitrations may include disputes where the violation would refer to the provisions of a treaty (a situation we previously referred to as 'the reversed umbrella clause'[54]).

54. For an account of the reverse umbrella clause, *see* C. Leaua, 'The Reverse Umbrella Clause: A Note in the Quest for the Conceptualization of Another Elephant in the Room', Chapter 74 in *Reflections on International Arbitration: Essays in Honour of Professor George Bermann*, Julie Bédard, Patrick W. Pearsall (eds), Juris, 2022, and C. Leaua, 'Contractual Requirements for

## §1.04 CONCLUSION

In our analysis of the recent trends in nature markets, we see a reconceptualization of the relationship between economics' notions of capital and money, on the one hand, and the ethical and legal values entailed in nature protection, on the other.

Arbitration maintains its classic advantages also in the new context of nature markets, which have a particular field of manifestation in this case, due to the need to approach in an interdisciplinary view the legal, economic and scientific environmental aspects of the potential disputes.

On the other hand, one can also note that nowadays overall litigious approach to environmental protection and the new developments of the nature markets, which are not yet enjoying a completely updated and internationally harmonized legislation, are prone to generate a number of new trends in the future development of commercial arbitration. Among such potential trends, the most significant ones we see are with regard to the pressure for the participation of non-signatories and the potential migration of the cases typically addressed in investment arbitration to commercial arbitration.

---

Environmental Compliance in Agreements with State and State Entities and Arbitration', Chapter in *Dispute Resolution and Climate Change: The Paris Agreement and Beyond*, W. Miles (ed.), International Chamber of Commerce in Paris, 2017.

CHAPTER 2

# ESG and International Arbitration: General Considerations

*Patrick Thieffry*

As appears from the above contributions, ESG (environmental, social, and corporate governance) is not, or is no longer, a soft-law concept of limited interest to lawyers. This is also true for arbitration. It is not only that the very practice of arbitration is increasingly involving itself with ESG and, for instance, as put by the Campaign for Greener Arbitrations, 'driving sustainable change in arbitration'.[1] Beyond such obvious but challenging trends[2] and looking at the disputes submitted to arbitration, duties and liabilities arise for the private sector. The stakes in international dispute resolution are no longer confined to the traditional bilateral sphere of private relationships as a result of the fact that sustainable finance strategy seeks to re-orient investments towards more sustainable technologies and businesses.[3] As far as international arbitration is concerned, this suggests two preliminary comments.

*First*, that sustainable finance strategy is pursued in a number of countries with the same line of thought, that of the Task-force on Climate-Related Financial Disclosures (TCFD)[4] created under the auspices of the G20's Financial Stability Board to help organizations assess climate change impacts on their financial situations and to disclose relevant information.[5] ESG-purpose transparency instruments are thus extensions of general corporate disclosure duties, and as such, they increasingly trigger

1. https://www.greenerarbitrations.com/ (accessed on 3 May 2023).
2. *See* below Chapter 6.
3. *See* EU Commission Communication of 6 July 2021 *Strategy for Financing the Transition to a Sustainable Economy*, COM(2021) 390 final.
4. FSB-TCFD (2022) About: Task-force on climate-related financial disclosures (TCFD), Task-force on Climate-Related Financial Disclosures (https://www.fsb-tcfd.org/about/ (accessed on 23 January 2023).
5. FSB (2018) About the FSB, Financial Stability Board (https://www.fsb.org/about/ (accessed on 23 January 2023)).

potential liabilities for large or listed corporations and for participants in financial markets such as insurance companies, investment funds, and financial consultants, as well as for their directors and officers in potentially many countries, and in particular in Switzerland as well as in the European Union, but also in the United States.[6]

In Switzerland, the Federal Council's Ordinance on Climate Disclosures of 23 November 2022[7] requires listed companies and those supervised under financial market regulations of a certain size[8] to prepare reports on climate information as of 1 January 2024.[9] As per the principle of 'double materiality', such a report must cover financial risks the company incurs as a result of its climate-related activities 'outside-in' and the climate impact of its activities 'inside-out'. Perhaps even more significantly, the company must adopt and implement 'a transition plan that is comparable with the Swiss climate goals' with reduction targets for its direct and indirect emissions and describe how it intends to implement that transition plan.[10]

In the European Union, under the Corporate Sustainability Reporting Directive (CSRD), large companies must likewise disclose both the environmental impacts of sustainability issues on their activities 'outside-in' and the impacts of their activities on the public and the environment 'inside-out', following the principle of 'double materiality'.[11] The Sustainable Finance Disclosure Regulation (SFDR) requires financial market operators to support the credibility of claims promoting allegedly sustainable investments.[12] Such disclosures are now improved by sustainability transparency instruments which aim at their coherence and sufficiency. The Taxonomy Regulation seeks a level-playing field through a coherent classification of activities contributing substantially to sustainability objectives.[13] A proposed Sustainability Due Diligence Directive (CS3D) would improve their sufficiency by setting forth a framework for investigation, verification and publication of the impacts of a company's activity on

6. It has been suggested that there could be a common law duty of care to exercise human rights due diligence: Doug Cassel, Outlining the Case for a Common Law Duty of Care of Business to Exercise Human Rights Due Diligence, *Business and Human Rights Journal*, 1 (2016), p. 179 DOI: 10.1017/bhj.2016.15.
7. https://www.newsd.admin.ch/newsd/message/attachments/74006.pdf.
8. Public companies, banks and insurance companies with 500 or more employees and at least CHF 20 million in total assets or more than CHF 40 million in turnover must report publicly on climate issues.
9. Interestingly, a majority of Swiss cantons had rejected a 'Swiss Responsible Business Initiative' (RBI) that would have introduced binding due diligence obligations and a corresponding liability for violations of business human rights for certain internationally active corporations domiciled in Switzerland (*see* Niklaus Zaugg & Alex Bardin, 'Business Human Rights – A New Field of Activity for Arbitration', ASA Bull 1 (2021), 109) DOI: 10.54648/asab2021009.
10. https://www.admin.ch/gov/en/start/documentation/media-releases.msg-id-91859.html.
11. Directive (EU) 2022/2464 of 14 December 2022 amending Regulation (EU) No. 537/2014, Directive 2004/109/EC, Directive 2006/43/EC and Directive 2013/34/EU, as regards corporate sustainability reporting [2022] OJ L 322/15.
12. Regulation 2019/2088 of 27 November 2019 on sustainability-related disclosures in the financial services sector, [2019] OJ L 317/1.
13. Regulation 2020/852 of 18 June 2020 on the establishment of a framework to facilitate sustainable investment, [2020] OJ L 198/13. To characterize as sustainable, an activity must contribute substantially to one or more of six objectives and not do '*significant harm*' to any such objectives.

sustainable development throughout its value chain,[14] not to mention the several already existing sector-specific duty of diligence legal requirements applicable to minerals from conflict zones,[15] certain commodities and products associated with deforestation and forest degradation,[16] and batteries and waste batteries.[17]

The US *Securities and Exchange Commission* is likewise considering amendments to its rules that would require subject companies to provide certain climate-related information in their registration statements and annual reports, such as climate-related risks that are reasonably likely to have a material impact on the corporate business, results of operations or financial condition, its greenhouse gas (GHG) emissions, and certain climate-related financial metrics.[18]

The fact that these developments may seem recent and focused on climate issues ought not to be misunderstood: some have a much broader ambit, and, in any event, ESG factors also concern the subject matter of environmental, social and other laws that have been adopted and implemented over the years. Needless to be recalled, Switzerland ratified the European Convention on Human Rights (ECHR) in 1974.

*Second*, under the above-mentioned EU Taxonomy Regulation, allegedly sustainable activities must not contribute substantially to one or more of the six listed environmental objectives[19] and do 'no significant harm' to any such objectives. They also have to comply with minimum safeguards, including the OECD Guidelines for Multinational Enterprises[20] and the UN Guiding Principles on Business and Human Rights (UNGPs).[21] In a most relevant way to the arbitration community, the UNGPs contemplate access to effective remedies for affected persons through judicial, administrative, legislative or other appropriate means, including State or '*non-State-based non-judicial grievance mechanisms*' and access to justice. Hence, should a company

14. Proposal for a directive on Corporate Sustainability Due Diligence and amending Directive (EU) 2019/1937, COM/2022/71 final.
15. Regulation (EU) 2017/821 of the European Parliament and of the Council of 17 May 2017 laying down supply chain due diligence obligations for Union importers of tin, tantalum and tungsten, their ores, and gold originating from conflict-affected and high-risk areas [2017] OJ L 130/1.
16. Regulation (EU) 2023/1115 of the European Parliament and of the Council of 31 May 2023 on the making available on the Union market and the export from the Union of certain commodities and products associated with deforestation and forest degradation and repealing Regulation (EU) No. 995/2010 [2023] OJ L 150/206.
17. Regulation (EU) 2023/1542 of the European Parliament and of the Council of 12 July 2023 concerning batteries and waste batteries, amending Directive 2008/98/EC and Regulation (EU) 2019/1020 and repealing Directive 2006/66/EC, [2023] OJ L 191/1.
18. Securities and Exchange Commission, *The Enhancement and Standardization of Climate-Related Disclosures for Investors*, 17 CFR 210, 229, 232, 239, and 249 [Release Nos 33-11042; 34-94478; File No. S7-10-22] RIN 3235-AM87. If the extent of a work were testimony to the seriousness of the project at hand, it should be noted that the document submitted to consultation is 490-page long.
19. Climate change mitigation and adaptation, protection of water and marine resources, pollution prevention and control, protection and restoration of biodiversity and ecosystems, circular economy.
20. https://www.oecd.org/corporate/mne/ (accessed on 8 August 2023).
21. UN Special Representative of the Secretary-General on the issue of human rights and transnational corporations and other business enterprises, *Guiding Principles on Business and Human Rights: Implementing the United Nations 'Protect, Respect and Remedy' Framework*, U.N. Doc. A/HRC/17/31 (21 March 2011).

publicize a unilateral offer to arbitrate human rights-related claims that are not settled through non-litigious grievance mechanisms, such a move would seem welcome.

This is all the more likely to result in disputes, including before arbitrators, that a synergy is developing between the three components of ESG, especially through issues pertaining to environmental protection, climate change and human rights. That synergy is illustrated in a most topical way in the so-called *Swiss Grand-mothers* who claim in the European Court of Human Rights (ECtHR) that Switzerland is in violation of the human rights of senior women because it does not adequately protect them from the effects of climate change to which they are especially exposed.[22] Climate change considerations, albeit they may not have been as present in actual arbitral disputes so far, are more or less directly relevant to several highly sensitive public interest areas: climate change may have adverse impacts on human rights, health, the environment or energy transition. Conversely, a wave of 'climate litigation'[23] relies on a wide array of legal bases, including increasing human rights and fundamental rights, in an attempt to trigger stronger responses from public authorities[24] and from the private sector.[25] In this respect, it should be noted that ESG standards are not merely formal voluntary commitments, soft-law or administrative requirements. There are many binding obligations involved, compliance with which may be sanctioned not only by administrative or criminal action but also by way of civil and commercial disputes.

Yet, ESG considerations as such have been infrequent in arbitral practice so far. Nevertheless, a large number of cases have been known to have environmental aspects and a few even human rights aspects.

In investment arbitration, a number of awards have relied on the foreseeability of the progressive strengthening of environmental protection, a well-known example of which is the award in *Methanex v. United States*,[26] or in the area of human health, such as with the *Philip Morris v. Uruguay* matter.[27] Awards related to energy transition and

22. *Verein KlimaSeniorinnen Schweiz e a v. Switzerland*, App no. 53600/20 (ECtHR, pending). In a nutshell, an association in which hundreds of elderly women are members and four elderly women complain of health problems which worsen during heatwaves and which impact their living and health conditions, and claim that the Swiss authorities should take the necessary measures to meet the 2030 goal set by the 2015 Paris Agreement on climate change and, absent such measures, failed to comply, in substance, with its positive obligations to effectively protect life under Article 2 ECHR and respect for private and family life and the home under Article 8 ECHR, read in light of the precautionary principle and the principle of intergenerational equity.
23. *See, e.g.*, the report issued in 2020 by UN Environment and the Columbia University's *Sabin Center for Climate Change Law* which mentioned 1,550 cases in 38 countries: *Global Climate Report – 2020 Status Review*, https://www.unep.org/resources/report/global-climate-litigation-report-2020-status-review (accessed on 8 February 2020).
24. Most noted were a few court decisions such as in the *Urgenda* case, *Hoge Raad*, 20 December 2019, ECLI:NL:HR:2019:2006; *see also Bundesverfassungsgericht*, 29 April 2021, *Neubauer, e. a.*, http://climatecasechart.com/climate-change-litigation/non-us-case/neubauer-et-al-v-germany/ (accessed on 15 March 2022).
25. *See, e.g.*, The Hague, 26 May 2021, *Milieudefensie et al. v. Royal Dutch Shell plc.*, ECLI:NL:RBDHA:2021:5337 (English translation: ECLI:NL:RBDHA:2021:5339).
26. *Methanex v. United States*, Final Award, UNCITRAL/NAFTA, 3 June 2005.
27. *Philip Morris Brands Sàrl, Philip Morris Products S.A. and Abal Hermanos S.A. v. Uruguay*, ICSID Case No. ARB/10/7, Award, 8 July 2016.

based on the Energy Charter Treaty generally tend to accept that, in the absence of other culpable behaviour of the responding State, its legitimate and rational measures do not normally amount to breaches of the investor's legitimate expectations which are qualified by the due diligence it is supposed to conduct as to the political, economic and social background in the host State.[28] It is even now accepted that investors may assert claims against host states based on their failure to adequately protect the relevant natural environment[29] and that host states may conversely make counterclaims against investors seeking compensation for environmental damages.[30]

In commercial arbitration, awards are known to have been issued in various situations relevant to environmental protection, most significantly dealing with warranty agreements in corporate acquisitions and sales of contaminated sites. Other cases concern construction and infrastructure projects such as waste disposal or valorization facilities, water treatment, solar parks, wind farms and hydroelectricity facilities, and yet others prospection, extraction, transportation, storage and distribution of natural resources.[31]

While arbitration remains scarcer in the Human Rights area, it is customary to mention the *Urbaser* case in investment arbitration[32] and, in '*commercial*' arbitration, the Bangladesh Accord on Fire and Building Safety, which was concluded following the collapse of the Rana Plaza factory building in 2013.[33] More recently, the ECtHR probably contributed to giving Human Rights a much larger stand in arbitration in *Semenya v. Switzerland* when it found that Switzerland committed a violation of the ECHR when the Swiss Federal Supreme Court failed to overturn a decision of the Court of Arbitration for Sport that discriminated against a professional athlete with differences of sex development who was required under non-State regulations to lower her natural testosterone level to compete in women's category in international competitions.[34]

In view of the ongoing legislative and jurisdictional developments worldwide, which can be expected to focus more and more on corporate governance as a means to improve ESG-related protection described above, an increase in arbitrations related to such objectives should be expected.

---

28. *See, e.g.*, Patrick Thieffry, *L'arbitrage au XXIè siècle face aux défis du changement climatique*, *Revue de l'arbitrage*, n° 3/2022, p. 899.
29. *Peter A. Allard (Canada) v. The Government of Barbados*, Case PCA 2012-06, Award, 27 June 2016.
30. *Burlington Resources Inc. v. Republic of Ecuador*, ICSID Case No. ARB/08/5, Decision on Counterclaims, 7 February 2017; *Perenco Ecuador Limited v. Republic of Ecuador*, ICSID Case No. ARB/08/6, Interim Decision on the Environmental Counterclaim, 11 August 2015, and Final Award, 27 September 2019.
31. Patrick Thieffry, *supra*.
32. *Urbaser S.A. and Consorcio de Aguas Bilbao Bizkaia, Bilbao Biskaia Ur Partzuergoa v. The Argentine Republic*, ICSID Case No. ARB/07/26, Award, 8 December 2016.
33. https://bangladeshaccord.org/ (accessed on 26 January 2023).
34. *Semenya v. Switzerland* App no. 10934/21 (ECtHR, 11 July 2023), ECLI:CE:ECHR:2023:0711 JUD001093421.

The question then arises if arbitration is, or could become, an appropriate forum for the resolution of such formally private disputes[35] which involve strong public interests. To a large extent, arbitration, being a voluntary alternative dispute resolution system, remains a consensual option to the parties. In the context of ESG-related disputes, which are of very significant general interest as well as public interest, consent to arbitrate will only be possible if there is a sufficient perception by decision-makers and stakeholders of its social acceptability. As was suggested years ago, failure to respect human rights 'can subject companies to the courts of public opinion' in view of 'what is sometimes called a company's social licence to operate'.[36] That social acceptability depends on procedures being perceived as fair and transparent and the public policies behind applicable substantive laws being honoured, i.e., on both procedural (§2.01) and substantive (§2.02) prerequisites.

## §2.01 ADAPTATION OF ARBITRAL PROCEDURES AND SOCIAL ACCEPTABILITY

As ESG-related institutional activity has been intense at the international level with respect to the investor-State dispute resolution system (ISDS) and, to a lesser extent, with respect to commercial arbitration (§2.01[A]), the Swiss Rules of International Arbitration appear to a large extent capable of applying to such disputes (§2.01[B]).

### [A] Institutional Approaches to ESG-Related Arbitration

A common way of apprehending the adaptation of arbitral procedures to private disputes in areas relevant to ESG is to take notice of institutional work in this respect. Indeed, for the past two decades, arbitration procedural frameworks have been improving as mechanisms to resolve environmental and human rights-related disputes.

The Permanent Court of Arbitration (PCA) is known to have administered a number of cases under its 2001 Optional Rules for Arbitration of Disputes Relating to Natural Resources and/or the Environment (the '*PCA Environmental Rules*')[37] concerning both State and non-State actors. The Hague Rules on Business and Human Rights Arbitration, which were presented in 2019, provide for the administration of arbitrations concerning disputes related to the impact of business activities on human

35. On this topic, *see, e.g.*, Niklaus Zaugg & Alex Bardin, *supra*; *see also* Gauthier Vannieuwenhuyse, 'Exploring the Suitability of Arbitration for Settling ESG and Human Rights Disputes', Journal of International Arbitration 40(1) (2023), p. 1 DOI: 10.54648/joia2023001.
36. UN Special Representative of the Secretary-General on the issue of human rights and transnational corporations and other business enterprises, *Protect, Respect and Remedy: a Framework for Business and Human Rights*, U.N. Doc. A/HRC/8/5 (7 April 2008), at 16-17, ¶ 54.
37. https://docs.pca-cpa.org/2016/01/Optional-Rules-for-Arbitration-of-Disputes-Relating-to-the-Environment-and_or-Natural-Resources.pdf (accessed on 7 September 2020).

rights.[38] Also in 2019, the International Chamber of Commerce (ICC) issued a report titled '*Resolving Climate Change Related Disputes through Arbitration and ADR*' (the '*ICC Task-force Report*'),[39] which verified the capability of arbitration in general and ICC arbitration in particular to offer adequate solutions, and explored 'potential procedural innovations and guidance for arbitration and ADR', in such disputes.[40]

Ongoing procedural changes in ISDS are also relevant. The first major step was taken in 2014 by the United Nations Commission on International Trade Law (UNCITRAL) when it adopted Rules on Transparency in Treaty-based Investor-State Arbitration (the 'UNCITRAL Rules on Transparency'), the application of which is promoted by the United Nations Convention on Transparency in Treaty-based Investor-State Arbitration, also known as the '*Mauritius Convention on Transparency*'.[41] UNCITRAL thus takes on board the publication not only of benchmark information but also of parties' and non-disputing parties' submissions, witness statements, expert reports, transcripts, or decisions rendered by the tribunal.

The International Centre for Settlement of Investment Disputes (ICSID) then amended its Convention Arbitration and Conciliation Rules (the 'ICSID Arbitration Rules') with effect from 1 July 2022. *Inter alia*, the ICSID Arbitration Rules as amended purport to alleviate the host States' defence burden by providing for the disposition of objections against claims manifestly without legal merit as to their substance, the jurisdiction of the Centre, or the competence of the tribunal (Rule 41) and a possible award of related costs to the prevailing party (Rule 52(2)). With a longer perspective in mind, the tribunal may grant a party security for costs in relevant circumstances (Rule 53). The 'observation of hearings' by third parties, as well as the publication of recordings or transcripts, become the general rule (Rules 65(1) and 65(2)). Recordings or transcripts of hearings will be publicized upon request of a party unless the other party objects (Rule 65(3)). In a less novel way, *amicus curiae* are provided for as 'submissions of non-disputing parties' subject to prior authorization of the tribunal (Rule 67).

Still ongoing is UNCITRAL's Working Group III discussion of an 'Investor-State Dispute Settlement Reform' involving major changes to arbitral procedure, many of which are similar or comparable.[42]

---

38. The Hague Rules on Business and Human Rights Arbitration, https://docs.pca-cpa.org/2019/12/The-Hague-Rules-on-Business-and-Human-Rights-Arbitration.pdf (accessed on 14 March 2022).
39. ICC, Resolving Climate Change Related Disputes through Arbitration and ADR, Report of the ICC Task-force on Arbitration of Climate Change Related Disputes: https://iccwbo.org/content/uploads/sites/3/2019/11/icc-arbitration-adr-commission-report-on-resolving-climate-change-related-disputes-english-version.pdf (accessed on 14 March 2022). The author was a co-chair of that Task-force.
40. ICC, Resolving Climate Change Related Disputes through Arbitration and ADR, para. 5.5.
41. https://uncitral.un.org/en/texts/arbitration/conventions/transparency (accessed on 14 March 2022).
42. https://uncitral.un.org/working_groups/3/investor-state (accessed on 28 August 2023). Much attention is given to the Working Group's Draft code of conduct for arbitrators in international investment dispute resolution, most notably its Article 4 on 'Limit on multiple roles' under which, absent agreement of the parties 'an Arbitrator shall not act concurrently as a legal representative or an expert witness in any other proceeding involving: (a) The same measure(s);

These several changes in the ISDS landscape align to quite some extent with those contemplated in the ICC Task-force Report. This is worth noting because the issue has been raised of a possible spill-over of the criticisms against ISDS to commercial arbitration,[43] which leads to the question of whether similar procedural trends should appear in commercial arbitration. Indeed, the ICC Task-force Report contemplates improvements relevant to both commercial and investment arbitration, which converge to strengthen the social acceptability of arbitration at large and, consequently, the willingness of stakeholders to arbitrate claims involving strong public interests.

At least three major trends can be noted. A first such trend, and a widely shared one, consists in alleviating the burden sustained by parties defending manifestly ill-founded claims, if not frivolous, by allowing their early disposition or by ensuring the possible compensation of procedural costs by the claimant ('security for costs').[44] A second relevant trend seeks some third-party information, at different levels between the mere publication of basic data, sometimes of redacted awards, to that of party submissions, expert reports, and hearing transcripts or even the publicity of hearings. A third trend furthers such opening on the grounds of third-party participation, such as by incorporating the practice of *amicus curiae* in arbitration rules and by venturing to allow their formal involvement as regular disputing parties, e.g., through the facilitated consolidation of separate arbitrations.

### [B] ESG-Related Arbitration under the Swiss Rules

It is worthwhile noting that the Swiss Rules of International Arbitration ('*Swiss Rules*', in force from 1 January 2023) are prone to accompany such adaptations, at least to a certain extent.

Early disposition of manifestly meritless claims seems possible as Article 36(2) which allows the tribunal to terminate the proceedings: '[i]f, before the award is made, the continuation of the arbitration proceedings becomes unnecessary or impossible for any reason [other than a settlement]' unless one of the parties, duly informed, raises 'justifiable grounds for objection'. Increased transparency may be agreed upon by the parties in derogation from the confidentiality provided for by Article 44, including a redacted copy of the award. And, while Article 27(7) provides that '[h]earings shall be

---

(b) The same or related party (parties); or (c) The same provision(s) of the same instrument of consent' (A/CN.9/1148, adopted at the Fifty-sixth session on 3-21 July 2023). However, its current work also involves several procedural items of great significance, akin to those adopted by ICSID. *See* Draft provisions on procedural and cross-cutting issues, to be discussed at the Forty-fourth session in Vienna on 9-13 October 2023, A/CN.9/WG.III/WP.231.

43. *See, e.g.*, J. Risse, 'The Future of Arbitration: A Poet's Prophecy', *Journal of International Arbitration* 36(6) (2019), p. 679, DOI: 10.54648/joia2019034; J. Grierson, T. Granier & S. Karsenti, 'Is Arbitration Helping or Hindering the Protection of the Environment and Public Health?', *Journal of International Arbitration* 38(3) (2021), p. 327 DOI: 10.54648/joia2021016.

44. Another device considered to alleviate the burden of responding states in the absence of arbitral case law is the establishment of an advisory centre on international investment law: *see* Draft provisions on the establishment of an advisory centre on international investment law, A/CN.9/WG.III/WP.230.

private', this is 'unless the parties agree otherwise'. Third-party involvement is contemplated by Article 6(4), which provides that '[w]here a third person requests or is requested by a party to participate in the arbitration proceedings in a capacity other than an additional party, the arbitral tribunal, after consulting with all parties and the third person, shall decide on whether to permit such participation and on its modalities, taking into account all relevant circumstances'. Such participation does not seem limited to *amicus curiae*. Public attendance at a hearing would be more problematic as Article 27 states that the hearing is 'for the presentation of evidence by witnesses or experts, or for oral argument' that '[h]earings shall be private, unless the parties agree otherwise'.

In addition, the 2023 Supplemental Swiss Rules for Corporate Law Disputes (the 'Supplemental Swiss Rules') are even more third-party friendly: they include a number of provisions which could be of use in ESG-related arbitration (assuming obviously that these or similar features would be offered *mutatis mutandis* in such a context). Those 'persons who may be directly affected by the legal effects of the arbitral award' (the '*Affected Persons*') are to be notified of the commencement of the arbitration (Article 2(1)) by appropriate means 'including publication in the Swiss Official Gazette of Commerce' (Article 2(4)), outlining in a concise manner 'the relief or remedy sought and the essential facts and background upon which the action is based' (Article 2(5)). Affected Persons may, upon request, be informed 'of the course of the arbitration proceedings', and the tribunal may, in its discretion, 'grant such persons access to parts of the file' (Article 5(2)). In addition, the Supplemental Swiss Rules recall that '[t]hird persons may participate in the arbitration proceedings pursuant to Article 6(4) of the Swiss Rules', with the tribunal taking into account 'the potential legal effects of the arbitral award on the respective third person' (Article 4).

This does not suggest that the Supplemental Swiss Rules could apply to just any ESG-related arbitration. Yet, the above-mentioned growing corporate governance-based environmental and human rights protection policies in Switzerland, like in the EU or in the US, could lead to corporate disputes. In addition, they show that the Centre could likewise administer ESG-related disputes under either the Swiss Rules or some variation thereof, institutional, contractual or ad hoc.

Arbitration may thus provide adequate responses in ESG-related disputes, allowing parties, counsel, and arbitrators to take advantage of a flexible procedural framework. However, parties' willingness to participate in arbitration may depend on the arbitrators' and the courts' treatment of the applicable substantive rules.

## §2.02 INTERNATIONAL PUBLIC POLICY, ARBITRATORS AND ARBITRAL AWARDS

The constant strengthening of substantive legal rules with ESG-related *ratio legis* that evoke public policy (§2.02[A]) raises the question of their handling in an arbitration context (§2.02[B]).

### [A] Strengthening of Substantive ESG-Related Legal Rules

There are thousands of international environmental agreements – multilateral, regional and bilateral treaties – and national laws.

For instance, the Federal Constitution provides that the Confederation and the Cantons 'shall endeavour to achieve a balanced and sustainable relationship between nature and its capacity to renew itself and the demands placed on it by the population' and that the Confederation 'shall legislate on the protection of the population and its natural environment against damage or nuisance' and 'ensure that such damage or nuisance is avoided'.[45] This is all the more remarkable that significant consequences were drawn by courts in other jurisdictions from comparable constitutional provisions, such as the German Federal Basic Law[46] or, most recently, the constitution of the state of Montana.[47]

Switzerland has been developing its environmental legislation since the 1960s.[48]A general Swiss Environmental Protection Act, which came into force in 1985,[49] is complemented by eleven acts and seventy-two ordinances in various sectors of the environment.[50] Switzerland provides for criminal prosecution for the most damaging environmental offences.[51] Most notably, a Swiss Federal Law of 30 September 2022,[52] which was submitted to referendum and approved on 18 June 2023,[53] sets

45. Federal Constitution of the Swiss Confederation of 18 April 1999, Articles 73-74, https://www.fedlex.admin.ch/eli/cc/1999/404/fr (accessed on 12 April 2023).
46. For instance, the German Federal Constitutional Court held that the protection of life and physical integrity under the Basic Law encompasses protection against impairments of 'constitutionally guaranteed interests caused by environmental pollution', and that 'the state's duty of protection encompasses the duty to protect life and health against the risks posed by climate change' (Bundesverfassungsgericht, 29 April 2021, *Neubauer, et al. v. Germany*, http://climatecasechart.com/climate-change-litigation/non-us-case/neubauer-et-al-v-germany/ (accessed on 26 August 2023).
47. A Montana State Court held in first instance that sixteen young Montanans have a constitutional right to clean and healthy environment which includes climate as part of an environmental life-support system, so that the Montana Environmental Policy Act may not prevent environmental assessments from including climate impacts of greenhouse gas emissions within or without the State when considering fossil-fuel extraction, treatment and consumption projects. *See Held v. Montana*, Montana First Judicial District Court, Findings of Fact, Conclusions of Law, and Order, 14 August 2023, https://climatecasechart.com/wp-content/uploads/case-documents/2023/20230814_docket-CDV-2020-307_order.pdf (accessed on 26 August 2023).
48. *See* Federal Office for the Environment (FOEN), Swiss Environmental Law (2022), https://www.bafu.admin.ch/bafu/en/home/topics/law/publications-studies/publications/swiss-environmental-law.html (accessed on 12 April 2022).
49. Federal Act on the Protection of the Environment of 7 October 1983, https://www.fedlex.admin.ch/eli/cc/1984/1122_1122_1122/fr (accessed on 12 April 2023).
50. *See* Federal Office for the Environment (FOEN), Swiss Environmental Law (2022), *supra*.
51. As FOEM puts it: '[o]rganised, international environmental criminals operate in lucrative businesses such as the illegal trade in waste or natural resources, including protected animal and plant species or illegally felled wood. What's more, international environmental crime often involves other forms of offending closely associated with organised crime, such as corruption and money laundering' (Federal Office for the Environment (FOEN), Swiss Environmental Law (2022), *supra*, p. 14.
52. *Loi fédérale sur les objectifs en matière de protection du climat, sur l'innovation et sur le renforcement de la sécurité énergétique (LCl)* of 30 September 2022, https://www.fedlex.admin.ch/eli/fga/2022/2403/fr (accessed on 12 April 2023).

targets for climate protection, innovation and energy security with a 2050-carbon neutrality consistent with the Paris Agreement as a countermeasure to a popular initiative that would have pursued even more ambitious objectives.[54]

In all of these respects, Switzerland does not differ from other countries, at least developed countries, to any significant extent.[55]

The magnitude of actual and potential legal risks these measures pose for businesses, as well as their significant normative strength, can be illustrated simply with two topical soft-law documents: the European Green Deal and the UNGPs.

The European Green Deal is a legislative agenda that EU institutions have been pursuing since December 2019 as a 'roadmap for making the EU's economy sustainable by turning climate and environmental challenges into opportunities across all policy areas and making the transition just and inclusive for all', and as part of the strategy to implement the UN 2030 Agenda and Sustainable Development Goals (SDGs).[56]

As the Swiss Federal Office for the Environment ('FOEN') puts it, 'Switzerland and the EU share many of the sustainable development targets outlined in the Green Deal', and it 'may benefit from these new developments in the EU' even though 'some measures could lead to trade barriers, such as product rules, or pose particular challenges [...]'.[57]

The Green Deal contemplates revisions of environmental legislations which are bound to impact industries on three main grounds: (i) circular economy with more stringent requirements on waste or construction products; (ii) biodiversity with such goals as restoration of damaged ecosystems, net zero artificialization or net zero deforestation; and (iii) a 'zero pollution' ambition with respect to air quality, large industrial facilities or chemicals.

But it is climate change which is at the heart of the Green Deal. Its first spectacular achievement has been the European Climate Law,[58] which gave legal force to 'a binding objective of climate neutrality in the Union by 2050 in pursuit of the long-term temperature goal set out' in the Paris Agreement. Comparable to the US administration's policy in substance, this climate neutrality objective was thus made legally binding. The EU is working on a series of legislations entitled '*Fit for 55*'[59] because they

53. *See* Swiss Federal Chancellery, *Votation populaire du 18 juin 2023*, https://www.bk.admin.ch/ch/f/pore/va/20230618/index.html (accessed on 18 June 2023).
54. Office fédéral suisse de l'environnement, *Loi sur le climat et l'innovation: vote populaire le 18 juin 2023*, https://www.bafu.admin.ch/bafu/fr/home/themes/climat/dossiers/loi-climat.html (accessed on 12 April 2023).
55. *See, e.g.*, Patrick Thieffry, Handbook of European Environment & Climate Law, Bruylant, 2nd ed., 2021, 489 pp.
56. European Commission Press Release IP/19/6691, *The European Green Deal Sets Out How to Make Europe the First Climate-Neutral Continent by 2050* (11 December 2019).
57. https://www.bafu.admin.ch/bafu/en/home/topics/international-affairs/organisations/relations-between-switzerland-and-the-eu-in-the-area-of-the-envi.html (accessed on 26 January 2023).
58. Regulation (EU) 2021/1119 of 30 June 2021, establishing the framework for achieving climate neutrality and amending Regulations (EC) No. 401/2009 and (EU) 2018/1999 ('European Climate Law') *JOUE*, [2021] OJ L 243/1.
59. EU Commission communication of 15 July 2021, 'Fit for 55': delivering the EU's 2030 Climate Target on the way to climate neutrality, COM(2021) 550 final.

aim at a 55% decrease in GHG emissions by 2030 as compared to 1990 so as to be on the trajectory of the 2050-carbon neutrality ultimate goal.[60]

As to human rights, the UNGPs are a clear sign of their relevance to business operators. The UNGPs' three pillars, 'Protect, Respect, Remedy', call for business and arbitrators' attention, respectively: (i) the State's duty to protect human rights abuses by businesses through policies, regulation and adjudication; (ii) corporate responsibility to respect human rights; and (iii) access to effective remedy through judicial and non-judicial grievance mechanisms. Interestingly, the UNGPs were welcomed by business organizations as an alternative to hard law.[61]

In the much-observed matter of *Royal Dutch Shell*, a Netherlands' first-degree state court found that, while human rights cannot be invoked as such against private companies, their underlying values could be factored in the interpretation of the civil code's unwritten standard of care because it can be deduced from soft-law instruments such as the UNGPs that companies must respect human rights. On that basis, it ordered that the whole *Shell* group limit or cause to be limited the aggregate annual volume of all $CO_2$ emissions (Scope 1, 2 and 3) directly or indirectly due to its business operations and sold energy-carrying products to such an extent that this volume will have reduced by at least net 45% at the end of 2030, relative to 2019 levels.[62]

The mere evocation of the EU Green Deal or the UNGPs, two examples amongst many ESG-related norms or frameworks, suggests a strong underlying general interest, and this raises the question of the status of substantive ESG-related legal rules in arbitration.

### [B] ESG-Related Public Policy, Arbitral Awards and Arbitrators

Substantive ESG-related legal norms are generally articulated in legal contexts both nationally and internationally, and this raises the question of their mandatory status in arbitration. Most ESG-related legal rules are probably characterized as public policy for domestic law purposes in the sense that parties cannot derogate therefrom. However, in an international context, their legal strength is more questionable and indeed, their

60. As opposed to the 40% target that had been declared by the EU in furtherance of the Paris Agreement in 2015. For details, *see* V.S. Schlacke et al., 'Implementing the EU Climate Law via the "Fit for 55" Package' *Oxford Open Energy*, Volume 1, 2022, p. 1.
61. *See, e.g.*, ICC Engagement with UN on Business and Human Rights, https://iccwbo.org/news-publications/policies-reports/icc-engagement-with-un-on-business-and-human-rights/ (accessed on 11 April 2023). *See also* Douglass Cassel, The 'Hardening' and 'Broadening' of Norms on Business and Human Rights, *in* Lauro Gama, Maria Inés Sola and Patrick Thieffry (eds), Navigating the New Contents of International Public Policy, Dossier XXI of the ICC Institute of World Business Law, ICC Publishing 2023.
62. The Hague, 26 May 2021, *Milieudefensie et al. v. Royal Dutch Shell plc.*, ECLI:NL:RB-DHA:2021:5337; *in English*: ECLI:NL:RBDHA:2021:5339. The Court downgraded its order to a significant best-efforts obligation only with respect to the business relations of the *Shell* group, including the end-users, in which context it may be expected to take the necessary steps to remove or prevent the serious risks ensuing from the $CO_2$ emissions generated by the business relations, and to use its influence to limit any lasting consequences as much as possible.

possible characterization as 'international public policy' and the impact of such a characterization remains debated in case law and scholarly works.[63]

For example, could *Royal Dutch Shell* rely on some concept of 'international public policy' to avoid compensating 'partners' within its value chain that it would terminate after they failed to properly comply and report on their ESG impacts? Both the legal and societal environments are such that '[c]ompanies who are higher up in the supply chain may take the role of watchdog or impose certain conditions on clients and end-users.'[64] Should they do so, disputes would follow, including in arbitration in the context of established commercial relationships.

This could be considered in relation to the arbitral award or to the arbitrator.

Considering the ultimate goal of arbitration, i.e., recognition or enforcement of an arbitral award, is a legal rule related to the environment or human rights altogether utterly imperative or may its imperiousness vary? In other words, should these rules be assessed per se, absent any consideration of the parties' actions or resulting damages which they seek to apprehend? Or does their normativity as legal standards vary depending on the seriousness of the said behaviour or damages?

In environmental matters, administrative law, or more precisely what French scholars have called *lois de droit public*, are applied by public authorities operating under the legal regimes pursuant to which they were instituted. For instance, in situations involving post-acquisition warranties in relation to contaminated sites, a governmental authority or agency, such as the Environmental Protection Agency in the US, generally determines the nature and extent of rehabilitation to be performed by the purchaser and current operator who, in turn, seeks indemnification from the seller. Arbitrators may have to consider the impacts of such administrative decisions on the parties' contractual relationships but would not normally apply such rules directly.

Absent the involvement of such a public authority, legal rules in the ESG area may likely characterize as overriding mandatory rules (*lois de police*) because they pursue crucial objectives within their scope of application, irrespective of the rules of conflict of the forum or of the law chosen by the parties. Indeed, the proposed CS3D Directive currently under consideration by the EU legislature would provide civil liability in cases of certain breaches of the corporate sustainability due diligence regime, which civil liability would be 'of overriding mandatory application in cases where the law applicable to claims to that effect is not the law of a Member State' of the European Union.[65]

Other such legal rules may come under the traditional eviction mechanism of international private law because they seek to protect fundamental 'values', denying the application of the foreign law that would otherwise apply to a legal situation, such

63. *See* Maria Inés Sola, Lauro Gama and Patrick Thieffry (eds), Navigating the New Contents of International Public Policy: Compliance in Environment and Human Rights, *supra*.
64. Gauthier Vannieuwenhuyse, 'Exploring the Suitability of Arbitration for Settling ESG and Human Rights Disputes', Journal of International Arbitration 40(1) (2023), p. 1 DOI: 10.54648/joia2023001.
65. Proposal for a Directive of the European Parliament and of the Council on Corporate Sustainability Due Diligence and amending Directive (EU) 2019/1937, 23 February 2022, COM(2022) 71 final, 2022/0051 (COD), Article 22(4).

as that designated by the forum's conflict of laws rules or denying recognition and enforcement of an arbitral award.

Ultimately, the foundation of underlying ESG rules should be of paramount importance in determining their legal strength. The imperiousness of such rules' *ratio legis* may be decisive in this respect, as appears when comparing legislations on corruption and competition. On the one hand, in corruption or money-laundering matters,[66] the facts at hand may seem irrelevant to the outcome of the dispute: any such behaviours seem univocally unacceptable. On the other, it is arguable that all competition laws should not bring about similar responses. As was put by the Swiss Federal Supreme Court in *Tensacciai S.P.A v. Freyssinet Terra Armata*, it would be 'presumptuous to consider that Western, European or Swiss conceptions of competition law should obviously impose themselves on all States on the planet, like a panacea, linked as they are to a certain type of economy and regime'. Moreover, 'Swiss law itself recognizes that not all restrictions of competition are harmful and it removes certain goods or services from free competition.'[67] Indeed, some anti-competitive practices, e.g., vertical restraints, have less damaging effects than others, such as horizontal cartels seeking to delay the introduction of greener products on the market.[68] Similarly, ESG concerns may not call for a single straightforward treatment.

At first sight, a *loi de police* or a core value giving rise to international public policy concerns under environmental legislation or human rights may seem to call for a straightforward treatment. This may, however, deserve further consideration. For example, releases of different substances in the environment do not bring about similar damages or social disapproval.

Likewise, some types of disputes may not warrant similar treatment when considered against given ESG rules as others. This was illustrated by the ECtHR finding in *Semenya v. Switzerland* that, while the Swiss Federal Supreme Court's very limited review over arbitral awards may be justified in commercial arbitration where companies generally on an equal footing agree to resolve their disputes that way, it may be more problematic in the area of sports arbitration where individuals sometimes face very powerful sports organizations, so that their judicial protection ought not to be lesser than for persons who have a more conventional job.[69]

Rather than characterizing an environment or human rights-related legal rule as international public policy 'per se', it may have to be considered from the viewpoint of the entire legal situation at hand, including the facts giving rise to the dispute. For instance, it seems that not all unlawful transborder shipments of waste or releases of

66. *See, e.g.*, Arbitration and Corruption, ASA Special Series No. 47, eds, Andrea Meier and Christian Oetiker, Kluwer Law International 2021.
67. Swiss Federal Supreme Court, 8 March 2006, *Tensacciai S.P.A v. Freyssinet Terra Armata S.R.L*, Official Reporter 132 ATF III 389, http://relevancy.bger.ch/php/clir/http/index.php?highlight_docid=atf%3A%2F%2F132-III-389%3Ade&lang=de&type=show_document.
68. Alexis Mourre, Confirmation du caractère limité du contrôle des sentences au regard de l'ordre public de fond, en particulier du droit communautaire, *Cahiers de l'arbitrage*, n°2/2012, p. 393; Alexis Mourre and Ina Popova, Le contrôle de l'ordre public, *Cahiers de l'arbitrage*, n°3/2022, p. 875.
69. *Semenya v. Switzerland, supra*, para. 177.

polluting substances into groundwaters or surface waters can be deemed breaches of 'international public policy'. At the other end of the spectrum, the disposal of non-hazardous extraction or construction waste may not warrant the same level of reprobation. Thus, the application of relevant legal rules is subject to factual circumstances such as the nature (and danger) of the specific waste or substances or the ecological status of the affected environment.

A most perplexing example is that of emissions trading systems (ETS) used by many countries to curb the GHG emissions of the largest emitters, i.e., cap & trade systems on major emissions of heavy industries. ETS are the single most powerful instrument for climate mitigation where they are in use and, consequently, of paramount general interest. Switzerland has its own ETS,[70] separate from but linked to the EU's, and they are used in other parts of the world as well, such as California or a dozen Eastern states partnering within the *Regional Greenhouse Gas Initiative*, to curb GHG emissions of the main heavy industry emitters.

While they are thus a crucial general interest instrument, ETS are in a sense inspired by the polluter-pays principle, and thus implementing the microeconomics theory of externalities. Allowances are called '*carbon taxes*' by some and '*permits to pollute*' by others. In an attempt to mitigate hardships on EU producers from the strengthening of the ETS, a carbon border adjustment mechanism (CBAM) is intended to prevent 'carbon leakage' of GHG emissions embedded in imports by implementing a similar pricing.[71] CBAM is received in many non-EU countries as a 'carbon import duty', and FOEM notes that it 'could lead to trade barriers'.[72]

In view of the importance, on the one hand, and the flexibility, on the other, of ETS, it is unclear whether such an emitter would be deemed in breach of a public policy rule. Notwithstanding the crucial role of ETS as a policy instrument, it would seem debatable that a subject EU manufacturer or non-EU importer be deemed in breach of an international public policy rule while that policy consists in putting a price on its operations and it can regularize its situation by curbing its emissions or purchasing allowances on the market.

Overall, these examples show that the application of legal ESG-related rules depends on the type of policy instrument considered, the nature of the specific behaviour, and the risks to the ecological status of the affected environment.

A different issue is whether arbitrators, even before issuing an award, should respond in all such legal situations with the same level of curiosity and willingness to take action. This raises the broader question of the intensity of the jurisdictional

70. The Swiss ETS comprises fifty installations, with emissions totalling approximately 5 million tonnes of $CO_2$ equivalent ($CO_2$eq), to be compared with the EU ETS's 11,000 installations, representing emissions of around 2 billion tonnes of $CO_2$eq. *See* Federal Office for the Environment, Linking the Swiss and EU emissions trading systems, https://www.bafu.admin.ch/bafu/en/home/topics/climate/info-specialists/reduction-measures/ets/linking-swiss-eu.html.
71. Regulation (EU) 2023/956 of the European Parliament and of the Council of 10 May 2023 establishing a carbon border adjustment mechanism [2023] OJ L 130/52.
72. https://www.bafu.admin.ch/bafu/en/home/topics/international-affairs/organisations/relations-between-switzerland-and-the-eu-in-the-area-of-the-envi.html (accessed on 26 January 2023).

control, either by state courts or by arbitral tribunals, over legal situations in which ESG-related international public policy legal rules are concerned. When red flags of corruption or money laundering appear, the question arises whether an arbitrator has a duty to investigate, and one may wonder whether he should do so as well in the case of a major pollution, release of GHGs or unethical or hazardous work practice, to name only a few relevant situations. What if conclusive evidence is absent? Should they refer the matter to competent governmental authorities such as public prosecutors? Such steps may seem more natural to state judges than to arbitrators, yet arbitrators are increasingly entrusted with jurisdictional powers through state court restraints in controlling their awards when considering their setting aside, recognition or enforcement. These and other similar concerns are likely to become controversial in ESG-related arbitrations.

Absent relevant reported cases at this time, there may be a temptation to reason on the basis of the various positions known with respect to corruption and money-laundering practices. A most debated issue is whether arbitrators have duties to investigate potential misconduct, particularly when it has not been raised by the parties in the absence of conclusive evidence. The most vexing question is probably whether to refer the matter to competent authorities.

## §2.03 CONCLUSION

Because of the growing use of ESG factors, including by governments as policy instruments in matters such as corruption and money laundering, forced labour, and climate change, ESG-related disputes may well develop as arbitration's newest game field. However, as an optional alternative mode of dispute resolution, arbitration requires the consent of the parties to a dispute, and parties should only consent if they feel comfortable with the process and if it is socially acceptable to stakeholders. Arbitral procedures may thus have to adapt and become more efficient, transparent, and open to the public. Arbitration awards must also meet the courts' requirements if they are to avoid set-aside and be recognized and enforced. In this respect, the strength of the ESG legal rules applied in a case may be a factor, like in other areas involving significant public policy.

These concerns are likely to remain highly controversial in the near future.

# PANEL 2 Commercial Dispute Resolution: ESG *Ante Portas*?

CHAPTER 3

# Arbitration as a Means for Resolving Climate Change-Related Disputes

*Moritz Keller & Sunny Kapoor*

## §3.01 INTRODUCTION

Climate change is one of the greatest challenges of our time, raising crucial questions about the future of humanity. The growing consciousness and rapidly developing norms for protecting the environment and society at large from the harmful effects of certain economic activities are impacting global commerce. In recent years, environmental and social issues have given rise to ESG (environmental, social, and corporate governance) as a concept at the forefront of global and corporate governance. Accordingly, politics has been shaping this concept through constant regulation. The latest milestone was reached by the conclusion of the Paris Agreement in November 2016, in which the signatory States committed to combat the rise in the average temperature of the planet and which is considered to be the turning point in setting concrete obligations relating to climate change.[1]

In light of this commitment, the European Union has adopted the 'Green Deal' to increase the pace of the energy transition in the Member States, followed by a series of new regulations, e.g., the Taxonomy Regulation,[2] Regulation on sustainability-related disclosures in the financial services sector[3] or the Corporate Sustainability Reporting

1. *See generally Key aspects of the Paris Agreement* (United Nations Climate Change) available at https://unfccc.int/most-requested/key-aspects-of-the-paris-agreement (accessed on 17 December 2023).
2. Regulation (EU) 2020/852 of the European Parliament and of the Council of 18 June 2020 on the establishment of a framework to facilitate sustainable investment, and amending Regulation (EU) 2019/2088.
3. Regulation (EU) 2019/2088 of the European Parliament and of the Council of 27 November 2019 on sustainability-related disclosures in the financial services sector.

Directive.[4] The latest agreement of the United Nations Climate Change Conference in December 2023 underlines the raising awareness for climate actions and is said to signal the 'beginning of the end' of the fossil fuel era.[5] The political pressure to cut down climate-damaging emissions in order to pave the way for the energy transition increases. In view of these socio-political developments, it is hardly surprising that climate-related disputes have been on the rise over the past years. Climate change has ultimately reached the courts. Since the overwhelming majority of the publicly known cases have been brought before State courts, the question arises of how arbitration can be a means for resolving climate-related disputes. This chapter will highlight the key climate-related cases before State courts and the key legal questions related to those cases. It will then deal with the potential fields of disputes where arbitration could be a means for resolving climate-related disputes.

## §3.02 CLIMATE CHANGE DISPUTES INVOLVING PRIVATE ACTORS

### [A] State Court Litigation

While there are a growing number of ESG-related litigations arising out of international and domestic instruments against States, it is questionable how ESG disputes involving or against private actors should be resolved. Generally, States provide for some form of civil (e.g., tort) or criminal jurisdiction against private actors situated within their territory, which are being used to bring claims alleging environmental and related social harm, so-called Direct Climate Change Disputes. Regardless of the actual outcome of the proceedings, however, such public interest litigations against private actors further strategic goals of raising public attention to ESG issues through media coverage and consequently push for changes through legislation and policy. The chapter will provide a brief overview of some of the prominent Direct Climate Change Disputes, followed by a summary of the main legal issues related to such disputes.

#### *[1] Brief Overview of Prominent Direct Climate Change Disputes*

An example of Direct Climate Change Disputes which has gained significant attention is the case brought before the Dutch courts by several non-governmental organisations (NGOs) against a Dutch-British energy giant.[6] In this case, the plaintiffs criticised the respondent for its greenhouse gas emissions and obtained an order from the District Court of The Hague requiring the company to: (i) reduce its own $CO_2$ emissions by 45% compared to 2019 and by 2030, and (ii) do everything in its power to limit the $CO_2$

4. Directive (EU) 2022/2464 of the European Parliament and of the Council of 14 December 2022 amending Regulation (EU) No. 537/2014, Directive 2004/109/EC, Directive 2006/43/EC and Directive 2013/34/EU, as regards corporate sustainability reporting.
5. *See COP28 Agreement Signals 'Beginning of the End' of the Fossil Fuel Era* (United Nations Climate Change) available at https://unfccc.int/cop28 (accessed on 17 December 2023).
6. *Milieudefensie et al. v. Royal Dutch Shell plc.* (file number C/09/571932/ HA ZA 19-379; judgment dated 26 May 2021) (Appeal pending).

emissions of other companies in its group and of its end customers. The respondent's appeal is still pending.

Similarly, in 2015, a Peruvian farmer sued a German energy producer, alleging that by emitting greenhouse gases it caused a glacier near his home to melt, forcing him to take precautions against flooding and landslides. Despite the small amount claimed - EUR 17,000 - the consequences for operators in the sector could be significant if the court finds the respondent company liable. The claim was initially dismissed by the Essen District Court on the grounds that no causal link had been established between climate change and the greenhouse gases emitted by the respondent. It was argued that the consequences of climate change would continue even without the company's emissions.[7]

The decision is pending before the Higher Regional Court in Hamm, which has accepted the case on a prima facie basis and entered into the taking of evidence. The outcome will largely depend on the experts' answers to a number of fundamental questions, i.e., whether there is a serious risk of damage to the plaintiff's premises due to flooding and/or landslides as a result of the increased spread and volume of water in the lagoon, whether the defendant is contributing to the compression of greenhouse gas molecules and thus to global warming and whether the defendant's contribution to the rising temperatures is measurable and calculable.

A similar lawsuit has been brought more recently by four residents of the Indonesian island Pari against a French-Swiss cement producer. The plaintiffs claim that the respondent has been contributing to the rise of the sea level by emitting greenhouse gas emissions. The complaint is based on Swiss law provisions relating to the infringement of personal rights and redress for unjust harm. The plaintiffs are seeking compensation for damages already incurred, a reduction in greenhouse gases in order to prevent future damages and a contribution to protection measures on Pari so that future damage is prevented or is less severe. The case is currently pending before the Cantonal Court of Zug, which has recently granted the plaintiffs' request for free legal aid. This indicates that from the judge's point of view, the action does not seem to be lacking any chance of success.[8]

Further examples of climate change-related lawsuits in state courts are those brought by NGOs against German automotive producers. The civil actions have been formally lodged by the chairpersons of the NGO, who seek a court order to prevent the defendants from producing cars with combustion engines by 2030. The plaintiffs allocate an arbitrary $CO_2$ budget to each of the defendants, alleging that the continued production of cars with combustion engines will exceed that budget and prompt the German legislator to take measures for climate protection, which in turn will cause an adverse impact on the plaintiff's personality rights. All lawsuits have been dismissed in

7. *Luciano Lliuya v. RWE AG* (Case No. 2 O 285/15 Essen Regional Court) (Appeal pending).
8. *Asmania et al. v. Holcim* (Pending), https://climatecasechart.com/non-us-case/four-islanders-of-pari-v-holcim/ (accessed on 17 December 2023).

the first instance.[9] Two of the first-instance dismissals have already been confirmed by the appeals courts.[10]

### *[2] Typical Legal Issues in Climate Change-Related Lawsuits at State Courts*

Except in the case against the British-Dutch energy giant, the type of proceedings outlined above have generally been unsuccessful due to several legal hurdles one of which is the competence of the judiciary for resolving political questions. The Regional Courts of Stuttgart and Munich dismissed the actions against the car manufacturers on the basis that climate protection falls in the competence of the legislator, whose decisions should not be undermined by a court decision in a bilateral civil dispute.[11]

Another major legal issue from a German law perspective is the causal link between the event giving rise to the alleged damage and the loss resulting from that event. The standard under German law applied to establish the causal link is the so-called *conditio sine qua non* test (or '*but for test*'). Under this standard, an event is deemed to have caused the alleged damages if, without it, the said damages would not have occurred. However, in climate change disputes, the fact that there is no individual person responsible for causing climate change makes it exceedingly difficult for a claimant to prove a direct causal link between greenhouse gas emissions and the harm caused.[12] Accordingly, the Higher Regional Court Munich stressed that the car manufacturer's share of the global $CO_2$ emissions only amounts to 0.2%, the saving of which would neither stop climate change nor avoid the alleged harm.[13]

Furthermore, the plaintiffs in the climate change-related lawsuits have neither been able to substantiate a current or future infringement of their rights nor a tortious action by the defendants.[14] Lastly, the car manufacturers comply with the current legislative requirements. Even if the plaintiffs succeed in substantiating a current or

9. Regional Court Stuttgart, judgment of 13 September 2022, docket No. 17 O 789/21; Regional Court Detmold, judgment of 24 February 2023, docket No. 01 O 199/21; Regional Court Munich, judgment of 7 February 2022, docket No. 3 O 12581/21; Regional Court Braunschweig, judgment of 14 February 2022, docket No. 6 O 3931/21 (262).
10. Higher Regional Court München, judgment of 12 October 2023, docket No. 32 U 936/23; Higher Regional Court Stuttgart, judgment of 8 November 2023, docket No. 12 U 170/22.
11. Regional Court Stuttgart, judgment of 13 September 2022, docket No. 17 O 789/21, margin Nos 25 et seq.; Regional Court Munich, judgment of 7 February 2022, docket No. 3 O 12581/21, margin No. 69.
12. Regional Court Essen, judgment of 15 December 2016, docket No. 2 O 285/15; Moritz Keller, Sunny Kapoor and Jacqueline Momah, *Climate Change Litigation: The Types of Disputes, the Legal Challenges and the Role of Arbitration*, SchiedsVZ 2022, p. 15. *See also* Philipp Semmelmayer, *Climate Change and the German Law of Torts*, German Law Journal, 2021, Volume 22, Issue (8), pp. 1569-1582 DOI: 10.1017/glj.2021.76.
13. Higher Regional Court München, judgment of 12 October 2023, docket No. 32 U 936/23, margin No. 89.
14. Regional Court Stuttgart, judgment of 13 September 2022, docket No. 17 O 789/21, margin No. 20; Regional Court Detmold, judgment of 24 February 2023, docket No. 01 O 199/21, margin No. 17; Regional Court Munich, judgment of 7 February 2022, docket No. 3 O 12581/21, margin No. 58.

future infringement of their rights, the car manufacturers' actions are justified on the grounds of the principle of legitimate expectations.[15]

### [B] Arbitration

While domestic civil and criminal law are frequently used to seek redress relating to environmental and related social harm from companies, it is less common for arbitration and other ADR mechanisms to be used. This is simply because arbitration and ADR mechanisms are consensual, and it is rare for companies to voluntarily enter into such mechanisms when a dispute has arisen or is foreseeable.

One major example of an ESG-related dispute where arbitration was made available is the Rana Plaza tragedy in Bangladesh. Following the collapse of the Rana Plaza building, which killed more than 1,100 garment workers and injured more than 2,000, the Accord on Fire and Building Safety in Bangladesh was signed on 15 May 2013 as an agreement between global clothes brands and IndustriALL Global Union and UNI Global Union.[16] The agreement aims to establish a fire and building safety programme for workers in Bangladesh and covers 2.5 million workers in Bangladesh's garment industry. Article 5 of the Agreement contains an arbitration clause:

> Any dispute between the parties to, and arising under, the terms of this Agreement shall first be presented to and decided by the SC, which shall decide the dispute by majority vote of the SC within a maximum of 21 days of a petition being filed by one of the parties. *Upon request of either party, the decision of the SC may be appealed to a final and binding arbitration process.* Any arbitration award shall be enforceable in a court of law of the domicile of the signatory against whom enforcement is sought and shall be subject to The Convention on the Recognition and Enforcement of Foreign Arbitral Awards (The New York Convention), where applicable. [...] [emphasis added].

Following the events at Rana Plaza, the Bangladeshi workers' unions IndustriALL Global Union and UNI Global Union (the Claimants) commenced arbitrations under the 2010 UNCITRAL Arbitration Rules against a global fashion brand (the Respondent in PCA Case No. 2016-36) on 8 July 2016 and against another global fashion brand (the Respondent in PCA Case No. 2016-37) on 11 October 2016. On 17 July 2018, the arbitral tribunal constituted the two arbitrations and issued termination orders after the parties settled both sets of claims.[17] The brands paid USD 2.3 million to remediate unsafe conditions in garment factories in Bangladesh. These cases were administered by the Permanent Court of Arbitration (PCA).

---

15. Regional Court Munich, judgment of 7 February 2022, docket No. 3 O 12581/21, margin No. 68; Higher Regional Court München, judgment of 12 October 2023, docket No. 32 U 936/23, margin No. 75; Higher Regional Court Stuttgart, judgment of 8 November 2023, docket No. 12 U 170/22, margin No. 96.
16. Accord on Fire and Building Safety in Bangladesh, 15 May 2013 at https://bangladesh.wpengine.com/wp-content/uploads/2018/08/2013-Accord.pdf (accessed on 17 December 2023).
17. *Termination Order, IndustriALL Global Union and UNI Global Union v. X*, 17 July 2018, PCA Case No. 2016-36; *Termination Order, IndustriALL Global Union and UNI Global Union v. Y*, 17 July 2018, PCA Case No. 2016-37.

## §3.03 INDIRECT CLIMATE CHANGE DISPUTES IN THE CONTEXT OF ARBITRATION

Indirect climate change disputes are usually commercial disputes between private actors, which involve climate change as an incidental or substantial issue. The contours of such disputes are difficult to define because such disputes are often resolved confidentially through arbitration or do not gain significant publicity due to their primary commercial nature. This chapter will nonetheless highlight potential fields in which Indirect Climate Change Disputes could arise in the context of arbitration.

### [A] Energy Transition Disputes

With the growing emphasis on ESG norms, energy transition is gaining momentum in global commerce. This involves the *mitigation* of harmful environmental effects of existing projects, but also the *adaptation* of existing projects, buildings and infrastructure to be climate friendly. This includes a host of commercial activity[18] including, e.g.: (1) funding, insuring and licensing of renewable energy; (2) decommissioning of non-renewable power plants; (3) adaptation of existing buildings and infrastructure, including with reference to the United Nations Framework Convention on Climate Change (UNFCCC) framework. Some of these contracts, which include arbitration clauses, will presumably give rise to disputes touching upon whether the projects achieve the desired objectives in a climate-friendly manner. For example, an office building owner is required to insulate the building according to new climate-friendly regulations, which leads to a dispute with the contractor who failed to meet the regulatory standard.

### [B] ESG-Compliance Supply Chain

ESG norms are being increasingly considered in the process of contract-making in the context of global supply chain. New contracts may involve clauses which require parties to comply with ESG norms and keep their operations climate friendly. Such provisions, which may be an effective mechanism to monitor ESG-friendly practices in the global supply chain, may also give rise to disputes.

18. See, for example, the claim from a Colombian public utility (Empresas Públicas de Medellín (EPM)) filed against a Spanish insurer (Mapfre Seguros Generales de Colombia, 'Mapfre') at the Arbitration Court of the Medellín Chamber of Commerce (MCC) to seek USD 1.6 billion in compensation for the collapse of a hydroelectric dam which caused a major flood. Water breached a blocked tunnel in the dam following heavy rain and several landslides in 2018, causing flooding which destroyed homes, bridges and schools and left hundreds of people homeless. But the dispute has been settled on 25 January 2022 after Mapfre paid almost USD 1 billion to EPM.

An example of this type of dispute is embodied in the German Act on Corporate Due Diligence in Supply Chains of 16 July 2021.[19] Its material scope is very broad, as it applies to companies with a registered office in Germany and at least 3,000 employees in Germany. From 1 January 2024, it will even be extended to companies based in Germany with at least 1,000 employees (cf. Article 1). It requires these companies to conduct human rights and environmental due diligence in their supply chains, i.e., by establishing a risk management system and allocating responsibilities within the company (section 4), conducting regular risk analyses (section 5), issuing a policy statement and establishing preventive measures vis-à-vis suppliers (section 6), taking remedial action (section 7), establishing a complaints procedure (section 8), and documenting and reporting (section 10).

The Act provides that any person who claims to have been violated in any of his or her rights under section 2(1) may authorise a domestic trade union or NGO to initiate proceedings to enforce his or her rights (section 11(2)). By doing so, the individual assigns his or her right to the competent trade union to bring an action before the German courts on his or her behalf. In such a case, it is conceivable that the German company might, in turn, sue its subcontractor in the victim worker's country of origin to recover the damages it has paid to the worker as a result of the proceedings in Germany. This is where the benefits of arbitration can be seen, as contracts between foreign companies and their subcontractors very often contain an arbitration clause. In this case, commercial arbitration would concern the subcontractor's ESG obligations towards the injured worker.

Also, in its current version, the proposal for a European Directive on Corporate Sustainability Due Diligence of February 2022 contains a similar mechanism.[20] Article 22(1) provides that companies may be held liable if they fail to prevent potential negative impacts or to remedy existing negative impacts associated with their activities.[21] This provision, therefore, provides for the direct civil liability of the undertaking concerned. Consequently, if a company is held liable under this Directive for the actions of companies in the supply chain, it could take action against the company directly responsible. As with the mechanism introduced by the German Act on Corporate Due Diligence in Supply Chains, these disputes will most likely be settled by arbitration, as supplier and buyer contracts often contain arbitration clauses.

### [C] ESG-Compliance Investment Disputes

Shareholder disputes can also have an ESG dimension when shareholders of a company decide to sue the company in which they hold shares for environmental

19. Act on Corporate Due Diligence in Supply Chains of 16 July 2021.
20. Proposal for a Directive on Corporate Sustainability Due Diligence and amending Directive (EU) 2019/1937 (COM/2022/71 final).
21. The Council and the European Parliament reached a provisional deal on the CSDDD on 14 December 2023 including the prerequisites of the civil liability mechanism under Article 22, cf. https://www.consilium.europa.eu/en/press/press-releases/2023/12/14/corporate-sustainability-due-diligence-council-and-parliament-strike-deal-to-protect-environment-and-human-rights/ (accessed on 27 December 2023).

damage. This was the case, for example, in the recent English High Court case brought by a minority shareholder, ClientEarth, which sought to sue the oil company's directors. The underlying claim brought by ClientEarth alleged that the directors breached their statutory duties owed to the respondent by acts and omissions in relation to: (1) the company's Energy Transition Strategy (ETS) published and updated between April 2021 and 2022; and (2) the directors' response to an order made by the District Court of The Hague on 26 May 2021 ('Dutch Order') in the case *Milieudefensie v. Royal Dutch Shell plc.*

Regarding the company's ETC, the High Court held that it belongs to the directors of the company to act in the company's best interests. According to the court, the Board takes into account a range of competing considerations in managing the company, a competence that the court was 'ill-equipped to interfere' with.[22] With respect to the Dutch Order, the High Court found that there is no provision in English law requiring the directors to comply with an order of a foreign court.

The Court also ruled that ClientEarth did not act in good faith towards the respondent in bringing that claim. It stated: 'Where the primary purpose of bringing the claim is an ulterior motive in the form of advancing ClientEarth's own policy agenda with the consequence that, but for that purpose, the claim would not have been brought at all, it will not have been brought in good faith.'[23] The English Court found that ClientEarth was driven by such an ulterior motive and eventually rejected the claim. Although this case was heard by the national courts, it is conceivable for shareholders' agreements to contain arbitration clauses. In such cases, the dispute would fall within the scope of commercial arbitration.

Besides, in response to the increase in ESG obligations on companies, an anti-ESG movement has also begun to grow, particularly in the United States. On 23 August 2022, Governor Ron DeSantis, together with the Board of Administration, passed a resolution 'directing the State of Florida's fund managers to invest state funds in a manner that prioritises the highest return for Florida taxpayers and retirees without regard to the ideological agenda of the environmental, social and corporate governance (ESGES) movement'.[24] On 1 December 2022, the State of Florida announced that it would withdraw USD 2 billion worth of assets from BlackRock because of its ESG policies.[25] Arbitration would also have a place in the disputes that could arise from this movement. If companies are politically pressured to act against ESG, this will inevitably lead to disputes with pro-ESG stakeholders such as investors, shareholders, contractors, etc.

22. *ClientEarth v. Shell Plc*, [2023] EWHC 1897 (Ch) (High Court of Justice, Business and Property Courts of England and Wales).
23. *Ibid.*
24. Governor Ron DeSantis' Press release, 23 August 2022, https://www.flgov.com/2022/08/23/governor-ron-desantis-eliminates-esg-considerations-from-state-pension-investments/ (accessed on 17 December 2023).
25. Reuters, *Florida pulls $2 bln from BlackRock in largest anti-ESG divestment*, 1 December 2022.

### [D] General Commercial Disputes

Contracts which have no specific climate change-related purpose or subject-matter and may even pre-date the Paris Agreement nevertheless may be impacted due to issues relating to climate change.

Such disputes would include claims for non-performance due to force majeure events caused by climate change. The standard investigation into the *foreseeability* and *duty to mitigate or find alternative ways to perform* may increasingly involve an analysis of climate change. For example, if a climate change-related natural disaster leads to an underperformance of a supply contract and a consequent invocation of force majeure, the question arises whether the buyer could claim that the natural disaster was foreseeable or that the industry standard is to secure sufficient supplies despite the occurrence of natural disasters. The question of force majeure may also arise with regard to increasingly ruthless climate activist protests such as those carried out by the Last Generation, a group of climate change activists, that blocked airport runways and caused massive disruption and delays in air traffic in July 2023.[26]

## §3.04 CONCLUSION

As climate change has gained significance in socio-economic, political as well as commercial, it is becoming pervasive in commercial dispute resolution, directly as a central cause of dispute or indirectly as an incidental issue. After the wave of Direct Climate Change Disputes in the arena of state courts, we expect Indirect Climate Change Disputes to rise within the contractual relationship of the parties. As particularly contracts with cross-border nexus usually include arbitration clauses, the increasing significance of climate change and ESG will potentially gain more weight in arbitration proceedings.

26. Euronews, *Germany: Climate activists glue themselves to runways, causing major travel disruption*, 13 July 2023, https://www.euronews.com/2023/07/13/germany-climate-activists-glue-themselves-to-runways-causing-major-travel-disruption (accessed on 17 December 2023).

CHAPTER 4

# Commercial Dispute Resolution: ESG *Ante Portas*?—Observations from the Board of Directors' Perspective

*Isabelle Romy*[*]

## §4.01 INTRODUCTION

The acronym ESG stands for Environment, Social and Governance and refers to the criteria used to evaluate companies and assess their sustainability impact beyond a sole focus on shareholders' return. While ESG issues are not particularly new, in recent years, they have become a key concern for all companies, whether listed or not, in all sectors of the economy. The pressure on corporations to integrate ESG criteria into their business strategy, to act in a more socially responsible manner and to be more transparent about their actions is coming from all sides: employees, investors, shareholders, the general public, nongovernmental organizations (NGOs), regulators and legislators.

In particular, there is a growing expectation that companies will align their strategies and operations with the goals of the Paris Agreement on climate change, even if national legislators have not yet set mandatory and binding targets for them to reduce their greenhouse gas emissions.[1]

It is the responsibility of a company's board and management to decide which ESG issues are most relevant to the company's business, to consider and balance the opportunities and risks, and to integrate these ESG issues into the business strategy,

* I would like to thank Mr. Gaétan Girard, MLaw and attorney-at-law, assistant to the Chair of Law at the EPFL, for his precious help in preparing and finalizing this contribution.

1. Isabelle Romy, *Aperçu et portée des exigences légales en matière de durabilité environnementale pour les entreprises suisses*, in: DEP 2023 747, p. 750.

including emerging and potentially disruptive trends. In addition, proper risk management requires consideration of ESG-related legal risks. The extent and nature of these risks can be inferred and illustrated by analyzing the current wave of ESG litigation against governments, companies, and directors.

This chapter therefore provides an overview of the current litigation landscape based on a few landmark cases related to climate change in order to illustrate some of the legal issues at stake and their implications from the perspective of the board of directors of a Swiss company.

## §4.02 BRIEF OVERVIEW OF THE BOARD OF DIRECTORS' ROLE AND OBLIGATIONS UNDER SWISS LAW

### [A] In General

In a company limited by shares, the most common legal form in Switzerland, the board of directors plays a crucial role in the implementation and management of ESG issues.

Under Swiss law, the board of directors of a limited company manages the company's business unless it has delegated this responsibility (Article 716 paragraph 2 of the Swiss Code of Obligations (CO)[2]). Even in the event of delegation, the Board of Directors retains the nontransferable and inalienable duties set forth in Article 716*a* CO, including the power to conduct the business of the company, to issue the necessary directives, to determine the organization of the company and to supervise the persons entrusted with the management of the company to ensure compliance with the law, the articles of association, the internal regulations and the directives. The members of the Board of Directors also owe a duty of care and loyalty; they must perform their duties with due diligence and faithfully safeguard the interests of the company and its various stakeholders (Article 717 CO).[3]

### [B] With Respect to ESG Issues Specifically

The scope of the board's duty of care with respect to ESG issues is not precisely defined in the above-mentioned provisions and essentially depends on the nature of the company's activities and business. However, good governance practices and new transparency and due diligence duties imposed on certain companies are clarifying these contours.

2. Federal Act on the Amendment of the Swiss Civil Code (Part Five: The Code of Obligations) of March 30, 1911 (RS 220; CO).
3. Christoph B. Bühler, in: Lukas Handschin (ed.), *Zürcher Kommentar, Obligationenrecht, Art. 698-726 und 731b OR*, 3d ed. 2018, Article 717 CO no. 4; Jean-Luc Chenaux & Mathieu Blanc, *§ 15 Corporate Governance*, in: *Berner Kommentar, Das Aktienrecht, Kommentar der ersten Stunde*, 2023, Nos. 101 et seq.; Henry Peter & Francesca Cavadini, in: Pierre Tercier, Marc Amstutz & Rita Trigo Trindade (ed.), *Commentaire romand—Code des obligations II*, 2d ed. 2017, Article 717 CO Nos. 1 et 3.

The inalienable duty to exercise overall management of the company includes ensuring that ESG issues relevant to the company's operations, both in terms of opportunities and risks, are properly considered and integrated into the company's business strategy.[4] However, defining an ESG strategy and embedding it into a company's business strategy is a complex endeavor with many challenges. One major challenge is the rapidly changing regulatory environment, both internationally and domestically. As a result, practices that are voluntary today may become mandatory tomorrow and recommended or common practices turn into greenwashing. In addition, there is currently no universally applicable ESG regulatory framework, either hard or soft law, that companies can refer to when defining, managing and reporting on their ESG commitments and engagement, but rather a wide range and variety of guidelines, principles and recommendations issued by governmental bodies, private associations or NGOs.[5]

The board of directors is responsible for ensuring that the company complies with the law (Article 716*a* paragraph 1 nos 2 and 5 CO). In the area of environmental protection, in particular, Swiss companies are directly affected by numerous environmental standards. For example, the Federal Law on Environmental Protection (EPA)[6] imposes various obligations on companies, including the obligation to prevent pollution and to reduce it at source to an acceptable economic level, taking into account the state-of-the-art and operating conditions (Article 11 paragraph 2 of the Law on the Protection of the Environment). These regulations are well known, but the legal framework for sustainability, especially with regard to climate change, is developing rapidly in Switzerland and abroad. For companies with international operations, identifying and updating a comprehensive inventory of applicable regulations becomes a real challenge. Depending on the size and activities of the company, entire teams are dedicated to regulatory monitoring to identify the entry into force of new mandatory standards and to anticipate legislative changes that may affect the company.

In addition, the board must ensure that an appropriate system is in place to assess, manage and mitigate risks, including ESG risks.[7] Despite the lack of a coherent and stable regulatory framework, ESG risks can generally be grouped into six categories:

- physical risks related to climate change that impact the production of goods;
- reputational risks for companies that do not adapt their business model quickly enough or which sell green products and services without ensuring or demonstrating the veracity of their claims;

4. Chenaux & Blanc, *supra* n. 3, Nos 127 et seq.; Rolf H. Weber & Andreas Hösli, *Corporate Climate Responsibility – aktienrechtliche Haftungsrisiken für den Verwaltungsrat?*, RSJ 116/2020 605, p. 608.
5. Among the most prominent are those of the Global Reporting Initiative, the Task Force on Climate-Related Financial Disclosures, and the UN Sustainable Development Goals, which serve as guidelines for states and regional governments, but are also widely used by private companies to define and implement their sustainability strategy.
6. Federal Act of October 7, 1983 on the Protection of the Environment (RS 814.01; EPA).
7. Chenaux & Blanc, *supra* n. 3, Nos. 129 et seq.; Henry Peter & Aurélien Rocher, *The Normative Effects of ESG Expectations on Companies and their Directors*, RSDA 4/2023 453, p. 468; Weber & Hösli, *supra* n. 4, pp. 608 and 611.

- transition risks, i.e. financial risks arising from policy adaptation measures or the costs of technological adaptation;
- regulatory risks, such as greenwashing,[8] consumer protection, stranded assets and the impact on capital requirements;
- financial risks, particularly access to capital markets and credit;
- legal risks, including the risk of being sued or the target of a regulatory enforcement action.

The Swiss Financial Market Supervisory Authority (FINMA) has clarified the nature of these risks for financial institutions in its Supervisory Communication 05/2021,[9] stating that:

> For financial institutions, the consequences of climate change may lead to significant financial risks in the long term. For market participants, climate change poses physical risks, such as climate-related natural disasters and their associated costs. On the other hand, financial institutions may be indirectly affected by so-called transition risks resulting from, among other things, climate policy measures. For example, illiquid assets in affected sectors could be exposed to increased valuation risks on the balance sheets of financial institutions.

The definition of these risks can also be applied to companies in the real economy, which face similar physical, transitional, and financial risks.

After identifying the relevant risks according to the company's business model, the board of directors must ensure that these risks are properly assessed, in particular regarding their impact on the business strategy and that they are appropriately mitigated (*see* Article 961*c* paragraph 2 CO). More specifically, Articles 964*a* et seq. CO, which came into force on January 1, 2022, require public interest companies to describe in their nonfinancial report their main environmental and climate risks and how they are managed.

Failure to comply with these obligations may expose the company and/or its board of directors to civil liability actions[10] or criminal sanctions,[11] in addition to damaging the company's reputation and that of its directors and undermining consumer and employee confidence.

---

8. Recommendations have been issued notably by Swiss Banking and the Swiss Financial Market Supervisory Authority (FINMA) to enhance the transparency of ESG products and services. A proposal for a plan and measures to prevent greenwashing is expected from the Federal Department of Finance (FDF) by the end of August 2024, unless the financial sector implements effective self-regulation embodying the position of the Federal Council expressed in December 2022 before that time. In Europe, the Commission adopted a proposal for a directive on the substantiation and communication of explicit environmental claims ("Green claims" directive) in March 2023, which envisages detailed requirements regarding the substantiation and communication of environmental claims. This directive is likely to come into force by the end of 2024 and apply to third countries from 2027.
9. FINMA Guidance 05/2021 of November 3, 2021, *Preventing and combating greenwashing*, n. 3.
10. *See, e.g.*, Marie-Christine Kaptan, *Klimawandel – Haftungsrisiken und Handlungsbedarf für Schweizer Unternehmen*, RSDA 2022 586; Andreas Hösli & Rolf H. Weber, *Klimaklagen gegen Unternehmen, Internationale Entwicklungen und deren Bedeutung für die Schweiz*, Jusletter May 25, 2020, Nos. 18 et seq. et 41 et seq.
11. Article 325ter of the Swiss Criminal Code of December 21, 1937 (RS 311.0; SCC).

## §4.03 ESG LITIGATION RISKS

### [A] ESG Strategic Litigation on the Rise

As reported in other contributions, litigation is increasingly being used around the world by NGOs, activists, and individuals as a strategic tool to advance or challenge public policy, raise public awareness, create social change, and change government and corporate behavior.[12] The number of strategic climate cases has increased significantly since the signing of the Paris Agreement on climate change in 2015,[13] and so far, there are no signs that this trend will stop or change.

Furthermore, other ESG issues, such as human rights, access to water and deforestation, are also gaining prominence and prompting litigation.

Companies and their boards should monitor the ESG litigation landscape, even if they are not in an industry or sector at risk, for the following non-exhaustive reasons:

- Courts around the world are shaping public policy on climate change and accelerating the transition to net zero carbon emissions by forcing their governments to take stronger action to address climate change. While not directed at private entities, climate change lawsuits against governments are relevant to companies because they have the potential to accelerate the transition to a carbon-neutral economy and lead to the adoption of more detailed and stringent $CO_2$ emission targets at the national level, which will have a ripple effect throughout the economy.
- Actions against companies that seek to enforce faster reductions in $CO_2$ emissions can also change corporate behavior and accelerate the energy transition, particularly by defining the scope and extent of the duty of care that companies must exercise. This, in turn, will allow companies to better anticipate and assess their own reputational, compliance, legal and financial risks.
- Understanding the evolution of case law can help companies and their boards take appropriate compliance measures to avoid litigation, which can be detrimental to the value of the company.[14]

---

12. United Nations Environment Programme (2023); Global Climate Litigation Report: 2023 Status Review, p. 7; Joana Setzer et al., *Climate Change Litigation and Central Banks*, in: Legal Working Paper Series (ed. European Central Bank), No. 21, December 2021, pp. 9 et seq.; Félise Rouiller, *Le contentieux climatique contre l'Etat: Aspects procéduraux de droit public suisse et américain*, 2023, Nos. 201 et seq.; Isabelle Romy, *Impact of ESG on Legal Risks: ESG Litigation on the Rise*, in: Purpose in Corporate Governance, CEDIDAC, 2024, p. 45 (to be published).
13. Joana Setzer and Catherine Higham, Global Trends in Climate Change Litigation: 2023 Snapshot, Grantham Research Institute on Climate Change and the Environment and Centre for Climate Change Economics and Policy, London School of Economics and Political Science, 2023, p. 2. The total number of cases was over 2,300 in May 2023. Outside the United States, Australia, the UK and the EU remain the jurisdictions with the highest volume of cases.
14. *See* Misato Sato et al., *Impacts of Climate Litigation on Firm Value*, Centre for Climate Change Economics and Policy, Working Paper No. 421, 2023, available at https://www.lse.ac.uk/granthaminstitute/wp-content/uploads/2023/05/working-paper-397_-Sato-Gostlow-Higham-Setzer-Venmans.pdf (accessed on February 21, 2024).

- Monitoring ESG litigation hence enables companies and their boards of directors to better understand and mitigate their own reputational, compliance, legal and financial risks.[15]

In the following, we will review some landmark cases against governments (*infra* section §4.03[B]) and companies (*infra* §4.03[C]) to identify some trends and developments and formulate some observations in the form of lessons learned to date (*infra* §4.04).

### [B] Strategic Actions Against Governments

Others have described the main climate lawsuits against governments and corporations, and I refer to them and other reports to avoid repetition.[16] Suffice it to say here that several courts in different countries have ordered their own governments to accelerate the reduction of $CO_2$ emissions in order to better protect their citizens. Examples of such rulings include *Urgenda Foundation v. State of the Netherlands,*[17] *Friends of the Irish Environment CLG v. The Government of Ireland*[18] and *Neubauer et al. v. Germany.*[19]

At the supranational level, the European Court of Human Rights (ECtHR) is due to rule on several cases, including the case brought by the association KlimaSeniorinnen Schweiz against Switzerland for violation of Articles 2 and 8 of the European Convention on Human Rights (ECHR).[20] This case deserves more attention, not only because Switzerland is directly involved but also because it could become a landmark case, as the Court will determine whether the applicants can be regarded as actual or potential victims, within the meaning of Article 34 of the Convention, of a breach of Articles 2 and 8 ECHR by reason of the alleged failure of the Swiss authorities to protect them effectively against the effects of global warming.

15. Romy, *supra* n. 12, p. 44-45.
16. *See* references in nn. 12 and 13 and the other contributions in this volume.
17. The judgment of the Court of First Instance of June 24, 2015 as well as the decision on appeal by the Hague Court of Appeal of October 9, 2018 and the judgment of the Dutch Supreme Court of December 20, 2019 are published in English under https://climatecasechart.com/non-us-case/urgenda-foundation-v-kingdom-of-the-netherlands/ (accessed on February 21, 2024). For a detailed analysis of the judgment of the Dutch Supreme Court, *see* Romy, *supra* n. 12, pp. 15 et seq.
18. Judgment of the Irish Supreme Court of July 31, 2020, available at http://climatecasechart.com/non-us-case/friends-of-the-irish-environment-v-ireland/ (accessed on February 21, 2024). For a short summary of the judgment of the Irish Supreme Court, *see* Romy, *supra* n. 12, pp. 19 et seq., and for a detailed analysis of the judgment *see* Charlotte Renglet, *The Decision of the Irish Supreme Court in Friends of the Irish Environment v. Ireland: A Significant Step Towards Government Accountability for Climate Change?*, Carbon & Climate Law Review, Vol. 14, No. 3 (2020), pp. 163-176, available at https://www.jstor.org/stable/27076686 (accessed on February 21, 2024) DOI: 10.21552/cclr/2020/3/5.
19. Judgment of the Bundesverfassungsgericht of March 24, 2021, BVerfG, Beschluss des Ersten Senats vom 24. März 2021 – 1BvR 2656/18, available in German and English at https://www.bverfg.de/e/rs20210324_1bvr265618.html (accessed on February 21, 2024). For an analysis of the judgment of the Bundesverfassungsgericht, *see* Romy, *supra* n. 12, pp. 17 et seq.
20. ECtHR, *Verein KlimaSeniorinnen Schweiz and Others v. Switzerland* (App. No. 53600/20).

The applicants are, on the one hand, an association under Swiss law for the prevention of climate change whose members are women with an average age of 73; among them, 650 are over 75, and, on the other hand, four elderly women aged between 78 and 89 who complain of health problems, worsening during heatwaves, which undermine their living conditions and general health.[21]

In 2016, they submitted a request to the Federal Council, the Federal Office for the Environment (FOEN) and the Federal Department of the Environment, Transport, Energy and Communications (DETEC), pointing to various flaws in the area of climate protection and requesting the authorities to take the necessary measures to meet the 2030 goal set by the 2015 Paris Agreement on climate change (COP21), signed and ratified by Switzerland.[22]

In a decision of April 25, 2017, the DETEC declared the request inadmissible, finding that the applicants were not individually affected in terms of their rights and could not be regarded as victims.[23] On November 27, 2018, the Federal Administrative Court dismissed an appeal filed by the applicants, finding that women over 75 were not the only population group affected by climate change.[24] The applicants filed an appeal to the Federal Supreme Court against the decision of the Federal Administrative Court, alleging a violation of the constitutional guarantees of the rights to life and protection of private and family life (Article 10 paragraph 1 and Article 13 paragraph 1 of the Swiss Federal Constitution[25] and Article 8 ECHR).[26]

In a judgment of May 5, 2020, the Swiss Federal Supreme Court dismissed the appeal, considering that at the current stage of warming and in view of the objective set by the Paris Agreement on climate change, the plaintiffs were not affected with sufficient intensity required by Article 25*a* of the Federal Act on Administrative Procedure[27] and did not have standing to appeal.[28] The Federal Supreme Court further emphasized that proposals for the implementation of a specific public policy in an area currently under discussion can, in principle, be introduced through the democratic participation of Swiss constitutional law.[29]

On November 26, 2020, the applicants lodged a complaint against Switzerland with the ECtHR, submitting that Switzerland has failed to fulfil its positive obligations to protect life effectively (Article 2 ECHR) and to ensure respect for their private and family life, including their home (Article 8 ECHR).[30] They allege, in particular, that the

21. Press release ECHR 142 (2022) issued by the Registrar of the Court on April 29, 2022, available at https://hudoc.echr.coe.int/eng#{%22itemid%22:[%22002-13649%22]} (accessed on February 21, 2024).
22. Judgment of the Swiss Federal Administrative Court of November 27, 2018, A-2992/2017 para. A; Judgment of the Swiss Federal Supreme Court of May 5, 2020, ATF 146 I 145, para. A.
23. Press release ECHR 142 (2022), *supra* n. 21.
24. *Ibid.*; Judgment of the Swiss Federal Administrative Court, *supra* n. 22, consid. 6 and 7.
25. Federal Constitution of the Swiss Confederation of April 18, 1999 (RS 101; Cst.).
26. Press release ECHR 142 (2022), *supra* n. 21; Judgment of the Swiss Federal Supreme Court, *supra* n. 22.
27. Federal Act of December 20, 1968 on Administrative Procedure (RS 172.021; APA).
28. ATF 146 I 145 para. 5.
29. ATF 146 I 145 paras. 4.3 and 5.5.
30. ECtHR, *Verein KlimaSeniorinnen Schweiz and Others v. Switzerland* (App. No. 53600/20); Press release ECHR 142 (2022), *supra* n. 21.

positive obligations under the Convention provisions should be considered in the light of the principles of precaution and intergenerational fairness provided for under international environmental law. In this context they complain that Switzerland has failed to introduce suitable legislation and to put appropriate and sufficient measures in place to reach the targets for combating climate change.[31] They further complain that they have not had access to a court within the meaning of Article 6 ECHR, alleging that the domestic courts have not properly responded to their requests and have given arbitrary decisions affecting their civil rights, particularly by totally rejecting their specific situation of vulnerability in relation to heatwaves.[32] Lastly, the applicants complain of a violation of Article 13 ECHR that protects the right to an effective remedy, arguing that no effective domestic remedy is available to them for the purpose of submitting their complaints under Articles 2 and 8 ECHR.[33]

On April 26, 2022, the Chamber to which the case had been allocated relinquished jurisdiction in favor of the Grand Chamber of the ECtHR,[34] which heard the case on March 29, 2023.[35]

Together with *Duarte Agostinho and Others v. Portugal and Others*,[36] *KlimaSeniorinnen Schweiz and Others v. Switzerland* is one of the first climate change cases before the ECtHR. These cases deserve special attention as, for the first time in the context of climate change, the ECtHR is asked to rule, *inter alia*, on the standing to bring a complaint (who is a victim of climate change?), the protection offered by Article 2 ECHR (right to life) and what positive obligations the states must fulfill to protect human rights in relation with climate change. The ECtHR may, hence, play a decisive role in shaping the protection offered by human rights in climate change and, consequently, the future of climate litigation against states.

### [C] Strategic Actions Against Corporations

The number of strategic ESG lawsuits against companies has also increased in recent years.[37] The cases are diverse and include civil actions for liability (damages) and/or for injunction.[38]

#### *[1]* Milieudefensie et al. v. Royal Dutch Shell PLC

On May 26, 2021, the Hague District Court issued a groundbreaking ruling by which it directed the Shell Group to reduce its net direct and indirect greenhouse gas emissions

31. Press release ECHR 142 (2022), *supra* n. 21.
32. *Ibid.*
33. *Ibid.*
34. *Ibid.*
35. Press release ECHR 094 (2023) issued by the Registrar of the Court on March 29, 2023, available at https://hudoc.echr.coe.int/eng#{%22itemid%22:[%22002-13649%22]} (accessed on February 21, 2024).
36. ECtHR, *Duarte Agostinho and Others v. Portugal and Others* (App. No. 39371/20).
37. Setzer & Higham, *supra* n. 13, pp. 2 and 35 et seq.
38. Romy, *supra* n. 12, p. 55.

by 45% in 2030 (compared to 2019) worldwide, in line with the Paris Agreement and the imperatives of climate science.[39] The reduction obligation covers the entire energy portfolio of the Shell Group worldwide and the aggregate volume of all its emissions (scopes 1 to 3), regardless of the regulations of the states in which the subsidiaries are located and the energy demand. Shell has appealed the judgment of first instance, and the case is pending.

One of the interests of this judgment lies in the Court's definition of the duty of care expected of Shell in relation to the fight against climate change.[40] The injunction requiring Shell to reduce its net direct and indirect greenhouse gas emissions worldwide by 45% by 2030 (compared to 2019) is based on general principles of Dutch tort law, embodied in the unwritten and flexible standard of the "prudent and reasonable person." According to the Hague District Court, this unwritten duty of care must be interpreted on the basis of fourteen elements,[41] which include Articles 2 and 8 ECHR. The Court stated that although human rights are not directly applicable against Shell, they can be taken into account when interpreting Shell's unwritten standard of care.[42] The Court found that it is certain that the Netherlands is threatened by climate change, and it referred to the case of *Urgenda Foundation v. State of* the *Netherlands* to find that the protection of human rights includes the dangers of climate change.[43] Articles 2 and 8 ECHR protect Dutch residents from the consequences of dangerous climate change caused by $CO_2$ emissions, which pose potentially serious and irreversible risks to the human rights of Dutch residents and the inhabitants of the Wadden Sea region.[44]

The Court stated further that the duty of care of Shell must be interpreted in the light of international "soft-law" instruments, such as the OECD Guidelines for Multinational Enterprises and the United Nations Guiding Principles on Business and Human Rights (UNGP), which impose a (nonbinding) responsibility on companies to respect human rights and formulate policies accordingly.[45]

Although the decision is not final, the court's ruling on the scope and extent of the duty of care expected of Shell is likely to set a precedent and pave the way for further decisions of this kind, especially as legislators around the world are tightening up the duty of care owed by companies.[46]

39. Judgment of the Hague District Court C/09/571932/HA ZA 19-379, ECLI:NL:RBDHA:2021:5339, of 26 May 2021, *Milieudefensie et al. v. Royal Dutch Shell PLC*. The Hague District Court issued an unofficial English translation of the judgment available at https://climatecasechart.com/wp-content/uploads/non-us-case-documents/2021/20210526_8918_judgment-1.pdf (accessed on February 21, 2024).
40. *See* Esmeralda Colombo, Unpacking Corporate Due Diligence in Transnational Climate Litigation: A Planetary Perspective, ex/ante S1/2023 35, pp. 42 et seq.
41. Judgment of the Hague District Court of 26 May 2021, *supra* n. 40, paras. 4.4.1 et seq.
42. *Ibid.*, para. 4.4.9.
43. *Ibid.*, para. 4.4.10.
44. *Ibid.*, paras. 4.4.6 and 4.4.10.
45. *Ibid.*, paras. 4.4.11 et seq.
46. *See* the Proposal for a Directive of the European Parliament and of the Council on Corporate Sustainability Due Diligence and amending Directive (EU) 2019/1937, COM/2022/71 final, which must be formally approved by the Council and the European Parliament.

### [2] Asmania et al. v. Holcim AG

In Switzerland, four inhabitants of the Indonesian island of Pari supported by three NGOs (HEKS/EPER [Switzerland], the European Center for Constitutional and European Human Rights [ECCHR] and WALHI [Indonesia]) sued Holcim AG in July 2022 by filing a request for conciliation before the Justice of the Peace of the Canton of Zug. The statement of claim was filed in November 2023, and the case is pending.[47]

The plaintiffs argue that Holcim is the largest cement producer in the world, that cement production worldwide contributes to 17% of the direct industrial greenhouse gas emissions, that Holcim contributes its part to 0.42% of the global $CO_2$ emissions and that according to Holcim's own sustainability report, its $CO_2$ emissions have increased. They allege further that climate change contributes to sea level rise that threatens their existence and economic prosperity. Based on Article 28 CC[48] (protection of personality rights) and Articles 41 CO and 49 CO (liability for tort), the plaintiffs request Holcim to pay a proportional compensation for climate change-related damages on Pari to reduce its $CO_2$ emissions by 43% by 2030, and by 69% until 2040, compared to 2019 levels (or according to findings of climate science in order to limit global warming to 1.5°C) and to pay a financial contribution to adaptation measures on Pari.[49]

The claim against Holcim is seen as novel and unprecedented as it combines two approaches, i.e., the reduction of greenhouse gases and compensation.[50]

### [3] FossielVrij NL v. KLM Royal Dutch Airlines

In December 2021, KLM launched its advertising campaign "Fly Responsibly," which focuses on aviation and sustainability. In this campaign, KLM claimed that its and the industry's path to the "net-zero ambition" consisted of fleet renewal, operational improvements, $CO_2$ offsets and "sustainable aviation fuels" (SAF).[51] The advertising campaign included the following slogans:[52]

> With Fly Responsibly, KLM is taking the lead in creating a more sustainable future for aviation.
>
> The aviation industry has the ambition to achieve just zero $CO_2$ emissions by 2050 and to underline this promise, we are developing our own path.

47. https://climatecasechart.com/non-us-case/four-islanders-of-pari-v-holcim/ (accessed on February 21, 2024).
48. Swiss Civil Code of December 10, 1907 (RS 210; CC).
49. https://climatecasechart.com/non-us-case/four-islanders-of-pari-v-holcim/ (accessed on February 21, 2024).
50. *Ibid.*
51. Petition filed on July 7, 2022 by FossielVrij NL against KLM with the Amsterdam District Court, No. 175, p. 58, an unofficial English translation of which is available at https://climatecasechart.com/wp-content/uploads/non-us-case-documents/2022/20220707_17244_petition.pdf (accessed on February 21, 2024).
52. Petition filed on 7 July 2022 by FossielVrij NL against KLM with the Amsterdam District Court, *supra* n. 51, No. 176, p. 59.

On April 8, 2022, the Dutch National Advertisement Code Commission ruled that elements of the KLM "Fly Responsibly" campaign violated the code's provisions on misleading advertising, especially those elements referring to "climate neutrality" or "$CO_2$ZERO."[53] The Commission noted, *inter alia*, that whilst the reforestation program in which KLM invests meets certain recognized theoretical standards (e.g., Gold Standard certification), there exist doubts in practice and amongst experts that emission reduction certificates purchased by KLM result in the full and permanent compensation "down to zero" of personal flight footprints in practice, as suggested by the campaign. Therefore, the absolute environmental claims of "$CO_2$-neutrality" and "$CO_2$ZERO" must be accompanied by sound, independent, verifiable and generally recognized evidence that, in practice, there is also guaranteed full compensation.[54]

On July 6, 2022, FossielVrij NL filed a lawsuit against KLM in the Amsterdam District Court seeking: (i) a declaration that the advertising statements made by KLM suggesting that flying can be or become sustainable are misleading and unlawful; (ii) a prohibition to advertise or suggest that flying, whether with KLM or not, can be done in a way that is "sustainable" or "responsible" from a climate change perspective, in any form or manner, to be made public; and (iii) a rectification of the advertisements, for example as follows: "The only way to meaningfully reduce the impact of flying on the climate and contribute to achieving the climate targets is by not flying."[55] As of today, the case is still pending.

### *[4] Climate Alliance Against FIFA*

In November 2022, Climate Alliance Switzerland and four foreign organizations and NGOs filed five independent complaints with the Swiss Commission for Fairness against FIFA. They alleged that the claims according to which the 2022 FIFA World Cup in Qatar was the first carbon-neutral World Cup were false and misleading.[56] In its decision dated June 5, 2023, the Commission approved the complaints. It advised FIFA to refrain from making unsubstantiated claims in the future, in particular, that the 2022 World Cup in Qatar would be neutral for the climate, unless it can provide, at the time of communication, full proof of the calculation, using generally accepted methods, of all $CO_2$ emissions caused by the tournament and, second, proof that these $CO_2$ emissions have been fully offset.[57]

53. Romy, *supra* n. 12, p. 25 s.; https://climatecasechart.com/non-us-case/fossielvrij-nl-v-klm/ (accessed on February 21, 2024).
54. https://climatecasechart.com/non-us-case/fossielvrij-nl-v-klm/ (accessed on February 1, 2024).
55. Petition filed on July 7, 2022 by FossielVrij NL against KLM with the Amsterdam District Court, *supra* n. 51, p. 139 ss; Romy, *supra* n. 12, p. 26.
56. https://www.faire-werbung.ch/de/swiss-commission-for-fairness-upholds-complaints-against-fifa/ (accessed on February 21, 2024).
57. https://www.faire-werbung.ch/de/swiss-commission-for-fairness-upholds-complaints-against-fifa/ (accessed on February 21, 2024). The full text of the decision is available in French at https://www.faire-werbung.ch/wp-content/uploads/2023/08/No_188_22.pdf (accessed on February 21, 2024).

Although the Commission has no power to impose sanctions, the "name and shame" effect of its decisions cannot be underestimated.

At the beginning of September 2023, Climate Alliance Switzerland asked the State Secretariat for Economic Affairs (SECO) to publicly condemn FIFA's behavior or even file a criminal complaint against it. The SECO refused to do so, as FIFA had withdrawn its allegations of climate neutrality.[58]

In addition, on July 6, 2023, the Consumer Protection Foundation filed eleven complaints, eight with the SECO and three with the Swiss Commission for Fairness, against eight companies, including Coca-Cola Switzerland, Hipp, Swisscom and Elite-flights, for misleading "green" claims in advertisements in violation of Article 3 of the Unfair Competition Act (UCA).[59,60]

### *[5]* ClientEarth, Surfrider Foundation Europe and Zero Waste France v. Danone

ESG litigation is not only about climate warming but also expands to other environment-related issues. For instance, in January 2023, three environmental groups filed a lawsuit in the Paris Tribunal Judiciaire against Danone, the producer of Evian water and Activia yoghurts, regarding the use of plastic packaging. The plaintiffs argue that Danone is not doing enough to reduce its plastic footprint and that its "vigilance plan" is completely silent on plastics despite Danone being one of the world's top ten plastic polluters.[61]

The case is pending and likely to become an important milestone in plastics-related litigation since it differs from most ESG cases insofar as the plaintiffs do not seek damages for harm done or for misleading claims on sustainability but want to demonstrate that the company's overall strategy on plastic is not sufficient given the global risks to health and the environment posed by plastic waste.

## §4.04 SOME LESSONS LEARNED (TO DATE)

These few examples illustrate a global phenomenon—the use of litigation as a strategic tool—that is growing in the face of the climate emergency and the responses of governments and businesses, which are deemed insufficient. A review of recent court rulings in Europe and of lawsuits against states and companies allows us to make the following observations in the form of lessons learned to date, with the caveat that they may not be definitive in this rapidly evolving context.

---

58. https://avocatclimat.ch/greenwashing-de-la-fifa-la-frilosite-de-la-confederation/#pll_switcher (accessed on February 21, 2024).
59. Federal Act of December 19, 1986 on Unfair Competition (RS 241; UCA).
60. https://www.konsumentenschutz.ch/medienmitteilungen/zwoelf-beschwerden-wegen-green washing/ (accessed on February 21, 2024).
61. Romy, *supra* n. 12, p. 25; https://www.zerowastefrance.org/zero-waste-france-et-2-autres-ongs-assignent-danone-en-justice-pour-son-utilisation-de-plastique/ (accessed on February 21, 2024).

### [A] Compliance with Mandatory Public Law Is Necessary but Not Sufficient

Compliance with the law and regulation is not sufficient to shield a company from liability or injunction claims, as liability can be based on unspecified duty of diligence, voluntary commitments and expectations that exceed existing mandatory duties.

This was exemplified in the judgment of May 26, 2021, in the case *Milieudefensie et al. v. Royal Dutch Shell PLC:* for the first time, a parent company was obliged to decarbonize all the companies it controls, regardless of the regulations of the states in which the subsidiaries are located and regardless of the energy demand.[62] Although Shell has no direct legal human rights obligations, its human rights responsibilities influenced the court's interpretation of the company's duty of care. In particular, the court referred to the UNGP, a global standard consolidating existing international human rights law, which requires companies to identify, prevent and address human rights impacts related to their activities.[63]

Expectations, voluntary commitments, and soft law are therefore becoming increasingly important in that they shape the scope and extent of the indeterminate duty of care or due diligence imposed on companies and supplement the lack of clear substantive obligations in national legislation.

### [B] Voluntary or Mandatory Disclosures Fuels Litigation

Transparency of information, particularly in companies' sustainability reports, fuels litigation, as the companies' strategy and disclosures are scrutinized by NGOs, activists and regulators, who verify that companies' actions are consistent with ESG goals and targets that they have voluntarily set for themselves. Plaintiffs often rely on these reports to sue companies over alleged failure to address climate change or over missed targets.[64] In this respect, the new nonfinancial reporting obligations enacted in Switzerland (Articles 964a seq. CO) and in the European Union (Corporate Sustainability Reporting Directive (CSRD)[65]) are likely to sustain this trend and provide new arguments for further ESG lawsuits against companies.

Although strategic ESG litigation predominantly focused on climate change so far, the scope of new reporting and diligence obligations is much broader. Transparency and access to companies' data might lead to the filing of strategic actions for alleged violations of due diligence in the supply chain, human rights, and deforestation. It is therefore crucial that claims made in sustainability reports are accurate and verifiable.

62. Judgment of the Hague District Court of May 26, 2021, *supra* n. 39, para. 5.3 in association with paras. 4.4.22 et seq.; Romy, *supra* n. 2, pp. 56.
63. Judgment of the Hague District Court of May 26, 2021, *supra* n. 39, consid. 4.4.11 et seq.; Romy, *supra* n. 12, p. 57.
64. Romy, *supra* n. 12, pp. 46.
65. Directive (EU) 2022/2464 of the European Parliament and of the Council of 14 December 2022 amending Regulation (EU) No 537/2014, Directive 2004/109/EC, Directive 2006/43/EC and Directive 2013/34/EU, as regards corporate sustainability reporting, L 322/15.

### [C] Board Members Can Be Held Personally Liable

Board members are being challenged and could be held personally liable for alleged failure to prepare for net zero transition. In the United Kingdom (UK), for instance, ClientEarth, which held shares in Shell Plc, lodged a derivative claim on February 9, 2023, against the board of directors of Shell with the High Court of Justice in London, alleging that Shell's board of directors had failed to prepare for the energy transition and to implement a climate strategy that is in-keeping with the Paris Agreement goal.[66] In substance, the plaintiff argued that Shell's board of directors is legally required by UK company law to manage risks to the company that could harm its future success, climate risk being the biggest of them all. Despite Shell committing to being a net-zero company by 2050, its interim targets and strategy to reach this objective do not align, and Shell's strategy would in fact result in a reduction of just 5% in net emissions by the end of the decade. Additionally, the board of directors' plans fall short of the 2021 Dutch judgment in the case *Milieudefensie v. Shell*, which ordered the company to cut its overall emissions by 45% by 2030.[67]

ClientEarth relied on two statutory general duties owed by the Directors, namely the duty to promote the success of the company and the duty to exercise reasonable care, skill and diligence.[68]

On May 12, 2023, the High Court considered that ClientEarth's application and the evidence adduced in support of it did not disclose a prima facie case for giving permission to continue the claim,[69] and ClientEarth was refused permission to appeal by the Court of Appeal in November 2023, bringing the litigation to an end.[70]

In its reasoning, the High Court recognized that the impact of Shell's operations on the community and the environment is a matter for the directors to balance.[71] However, their response to the business risks to Shell associated with climate change is part of the decision-making process by which the directors manage Shell's business. While there are fundamental disagreements between ClientEarth and Shell's directors as to the right way to achieve the net zero 2050 targets that Shell has set itself, the law respects the autonomy of the directors to make decisions on commercial matters and their judgement as to how best to achieve outcomes that are in the best interests of their members as a whole. According to the Court, the evidence falls far short of establishing

66. https://www.clientearth.org/latest/press-office/press/court-fails-to-engage-with-key-climate-risk-arguments-in-shell-directors-case-dismissal/ (accessed on 21 February 2024).
67. https://www.clientearth.org/latest/news/we-re-taking-legal-action-against-shell-s-board-for-mismanaging-climate-risk/ (accessed on February 21, 2024).
68. https://www.clientearth.org/latest/news/we-re-taking-legal-action-against-shell-s-board-for-mismanaging-climate-risk/ > 4 (accessed on February 2, 2024) (accessed on February 21, 2024).
69. The court is required to dismiss the application if it appears to the court that the application itself and the evidence filed in support of it, do not disclose a prima facie case for giving permission: *see* Judgment of the High Court of Justice of London of May 12, 2023, *ClientEarth v. Shell Plc and others*, para. 4, available at https://climatecasechart.com/wp-content/uploads/non-us-case-documents/2023/20230512_2023-EWHC-1137-Ch-2023-EWHC-1897-Ch-2023-EWHC-2182-Ch-_judgment-1.pdf (accessed on 21 February 2024).
70. https://climatecasechart.com/non-us-case/clientearth-v-shells-board-of-directors/ (accessed on February 21, 2024).
71. Judgment of the High Court of Justice of London of 12 May 2023, *supra* n. 69, para. 48.

a prima facie case that the way in which Shell's business is being managed by the directors could not reasonably be regarded by them as being in the best interests of Shell's members as a whole.[72]

The court also stated that ClientEarth's case completely ignored the fact that the management of a business of Shell's size and complexity requires the directors to take into account a range of competing considerations, the proper balancing of which is a classic management decision with which the court is ill-equipped to interfere.[73]

Although this particular claim failed, it is likely that directors will be increasingly exposed to liability litigation as transparency and reporting requirements are implemented around the world. As of January 1, 2024, Swiss law requires companies to disclose, among other things, their environmental impacts and transition plans towards net zero, as well as the associated financial risks and how they are managed and mitigated (*see* Article 964*b* paragraphs 1 and 2 CO). It is the duty of the board of directors to prepare and approve this report and then submit it to the shareholders' meeting for approval (Article 964*c* CO).[74] False statements in the reports, failure to prepare a report and breach of the duty to keep the reports are punishable under Article 325ter SCC (fine of up to CHF 100,000 in the case of a wilful breach and up to CHF 50,000 in the case of negligence).

In the EU, the new CSRD is based on the principle of "double materiality," according to which companies are required to report both on their impact on people and the environment and on how social and environmental issues create financial opportunities and risks for the company.[75]

These reports will provide valuable insights to shareholders and the public in general into the diligence with which boards manage ESG risks.

### [D] ESG Litigation Will Continue to Grow

The cases mentioned in this contribution are just a few examples of a global phenomenon that is growing in the face of the climate emergency.

Litigation has become a tool used by NGOs and others to remedy the inadequate responses of governments and the private sector to climate change and other environmental harms. Courts have become instrumental in shaping political and societal developments around sustainability topics in general and climate change in particular. The role of litigation in affecting "the outcome and ambition of climate governance" was recognized by the Intergovernmental Panel on Climate Change (IPCC) Working Group III in 2022, in a document approved by representatives of every Member State.[76]

72. *Ibid.*, paras. 47 et seq.
73. *Ibid.*, para. 48.
74. Romy, *supra* n. 1, pp. 759 et seq.
75. Corporate Sustainability Reporting Directive, *supra* n. 65, preamble Ch. 29.
76. IPCC, Climate Change 2022: Mitigation of Climate Change, Working Group III contribution to the Sixth Assessment Report of the IPCC, 2022, E.3.3, p. 46, available at https://www.ipcc.ch/report/ar6/wg3/downloads/report/IPCC_AR6_WGIII_FullReport.pdf (accessed on February 21, 2024).

ESG strategic litigation against Swiss global companies is also likely to increase, both in Switzerland and abroad, as a means to raise awareness and shape public policy.

As already mentioned above (*supra* §4.04[B]), although strategic litigation predominantly focuses on climate change, the scope of new reporting and diligence obligations is much broader, and transparency and access to companies' data might lead to the filing of strategic actions for alleged violations of due diligence in the supply chain, human rights, and deforestation.

This trend raises fundamental questions about the separation of powers and the role of the courts, whose activism sometimes bypasses, corrects or replaces the legislative process. In addition, judicial activism can potentially lead to greater unpredictability of the law, making it more difficult for companies and their boards to effectively assess and mitigate legal risk.

## §4.05 FINAL OBSERVATIONS

Regardless of the chances of success of similar lawsuits in Switzerland, companies, as well as their directors and legal advisors, should not ignore the developments occurring abroad and the decisions rendered by foreign courts. These cases and decisions are indeed relevant to Swiss companies and their boards, especially global companies, as they shape the expected duty of diligence and outline the legal risks that should be taken into account regardless of the company's place of incorporation.

As a result, proper risk management and good corporate governance require companies to monitor the litigation landscape to detect trends and reflect on the lessons learned, even though the outcome of many strategic cases is still outstanding and the regulatory context extremely dynamic. Changes in public policy affect the entire economy and the entire supply chain, not just the defendant's business, and may increase related financial transition costs.

In this context, the introduction of an arbitration clause in the articles of incorporation might offer protection against some strategic ESG litigation. According to the revised Swiss corporate law, which came into force on January 1, 2023, the articles of association of corporations may now provide that corporate law disputes be settled by arbitration proceedings in Switzerland (Article 697*n* CO). The same applies to partnerships limited by shares (Article 764 paragraph 2 CO in connection with Article 697*n* CO) and limited liability companies (Article 797*a* CO).

Arbitration clauses in articles of incorporation are, in principle, binding on all persons subject to the articles of association, i.e., specifically the company, the company's board of directors, the board members and the shareholders, as well as the participation certificate holders. As a result, if drafted properly, arbitration clauses may provide a useful tool to mitigate the risk of ESG lawsuits filed by persons subject to the articles of association, specifically by shareholders and participation certificate holders.

# Panel 3 ESG in Investment Arbitration: Status and Trends

CHAPTER 5

# The Energy Charter Treaty and Its Role in the Energy Transition

*Samantha J. Rowe**

## §5.01 INTRODUCTION

The Energy Charter Treaty ('ECT' or 'Treaty') turns thirty this year. Notwithstanding its relatively young age, in the eyes of many, it is in mortal decline. In recent years, the ECT has been subject to a barrage of criticism from Contracting Parties, civil society and the media, much of which has been focused on its role in the energy transition. Specifically, the ECT has been described as an insuperable obstacle to States' efforts to address climate change, both because it protects investments in fossil fuel projects and prevents States from adopting regulations that would 'phase out' fossil fuels in favour of cleaner energy sources such as renewables. This criticism has culminated in a spate of recent withdrawals and announced withdrawals from the ECT, calling into question its future.

In this article, which is based on the author's contribution to the '*ESG in investment arbitration: status and trends*' panel at the ASA Winter Conference 2023,[1] we critically examine the recent criticism of the ECT and, more broadly, its actual and potential role in the energy transition. We conclude – by reference to treaty language, statistics and case law that are often absent from the debate – that the ECT, in fact, has a valuable role to play in the energy transition, not least because it protects the very

* The author is grateful to Alma Mozetič, Diana Moise, Scott Morrison and Gökçe Uyar of Debevoise & Plimpton LLP for their valuable input and research support. The opinions and conclusions expressed in this chapter are solely those of the author; not of the author's firm or clients. Any errors are attributable solely to the author.

1. Swiss Arbitration Association Annual Conference 2-3 February 2023, *see* https://www.swissarbitration.org/events/swiss-arbitration-annual-conferences-2023/.

investments in clean energy that will be required to combat climate change. Finally, we examine the ECT's likely future in light of the modernisation process that is currently underway and the significant number of States that have announced their plans to withdraw from the Treaty.

The chapter proceeds as follows: §5.02 briefly reviews the ECT's origins, while §5.03 provides an overview of the criticism that has been levelled at the ECT by States, civil society and the media. In §5.04, we examine the language of the ECT and relevant case law to conclude that these criticisms are, in important respects, misplaced. Finally, in §5.05, we look at potential modernisation of the ECT and the likely outcome if the EU and its Member States proceed with their plans to withdraw from the Treaty.

## §5.02 THE ORIGINS OF THE ECT

In light of the current state of relations between Russia and the West, it can be difficult to recall that the ECT dates back to a time of great optimism in the aftermath of the Cold War. While the collapse of the Union of Soviet Socialist Republics (the 'Soviet Union') in 1991 marked a seismic shift in global geopolitics, it also presented unprecedented opportunities. This was particularly true for the energy sector, as it opened up the possibility of Western access to vast oil and gas resources in Eastern Europe.[2] Driven by the West's desire to strengthen economic ties with the East, the former Soviet Union was seen as a potential partner which could be brought closer to the West through economic - and energy - interdependency. The West would provide the capital that was needed in the East. In return, the East would provide the energy resources (especially natural gas) needed by the West.[3]

The European Energy Charter, initially proposed by Dutch Prime Minister Ruud Lubbers as the 'European Energy Community', was signed in 1991 as a non-binding declaration of principles. The Charter received widespread support, and counts among its signatories over fifty States in Europe, Canada, the US, Australia, and Japan. Before the ink had dried on the Charter, however, negotiations commenced which ultimately concluded in the signature of the ECT in Lisbon on 17 December 1994. The primary objective of the ECT at the time was twofold: to facilitate the transition of former communist States towards market economies and to bolster the rule of law to attract foreign investment in the energy sector.[4]

2. Thomas W. Wälde, 'Chapter 13. International Investment under the 1994 Energy Charter Treaty', in Thomas W. Wälde (ed.), The Energy Charter Treaty: An East-West Gateway for Investment and Trade (Kluwer Law International 1996), pp. 254-257.
3. *See generally* Cornel Marian, The State's Power to Tax (Kluwer Law International 2020), at 13-38.
4. Emmanuel Gaillard and Mark S. McNeill, '2. The Energy Charter Treaty', in Katia Yannaca-Small (ed.), Arbitration under International Investment Agreements: A Guide to the Key Issues (2nd ed.) (Oxford University Press 2018), pp. 32-33; Christoph H. Schreuer, 'Chapter 1: Investment Protection: Original Purpose and Features', in Ana Stanič and Crina Baltag (eds), The Future of Investment Treaty Arbitration in the EU: Intra-EU BITs, the Energy Charter Treaty, and the Multilateral Investment Court (Kluwer Law International 2020), pp. 1-3.

The ECT entered into force in 1998. At the time, few could imagine just how popular it would become. As of December 2023, it is the largest[5] and one of the most commonly invoked[6] investment treaties. It has, however, come under mounting pressure from States, civil society and the media in recent years in response to the climate crisis and increasing efforts to transition away from fossil fuels.

## §5.03 RECENT CRITICISM OF THE ECT's ROLE IN THE ENERGY TRANSITION

Much attention has been devoted to climate change in recent years, together with the need to address its root causes in order to avoid an increasingly urgent global crisis.[7] At the international level, these efforts are primarily reflected in the United Nations Framework Convention on Climate Change (UNFCCC) and the Paris Agreement, in which 193 parties committed to limit global warming to below 2°C and pursue efforts to limit it to 1.5°C, compared to pre-industrial levels.[8] The means for achieving this objective is the States Parties' 'Nationally Determined Contributions', in which each State sets out its own climate action plan to cut emissions and adapt to climate impacts.[9]

Many now recognise that a transition away from fossil fuels towards 'cleaner' forms of energy, such as renewables, is integral to global efforts to combat climate change.[10] For example, the most recent United Nations Climate Change Conference of the Parties - or 'COP' - held in 2023 marked the *momentous* conclusion of an agreement to transition away from fossil fuels in order to keep the global temperature limit of 1.5°C within reach.[11]

---

5. European Commission, 'Energy Charter' (undated), https://energy.ec.europa.eu/topics/international-cooperation/international-organisations-and-initiatives/energy-charter_en (56 signatories and Contracting Parties).
6. 162 arbitrations registered under the ECT as of 1 December 2023, *see* Energy Charter Secretariat, Statistics, available at https://www.energychartertreaty.org/cases/statistics/.
7. *See, e.g.*, IPCC, 'Urgent climate action can secure a liveable future for all' (20 March 2023), https://www.ipcc.ch/2023/03/20/press-release-ar6-synthesis-report/ (accessed on 21 February 2024); UN Environmental Programme, 'Facts about the climate emergency', https://www.unep.org/facts-about-climate-emergency (accessed on 21 February 2024); European Commission, 'Climate change', https://climate.ec.europa.eu/climate-change_en (accessed on 21 February 2024). *See also, e.g.*, Thomas L. Friedman, *Hot, Flat and Crowded* (Macmillan 2009).
8. Paris Agreement, Article 2(1)(a).
9. Paris Agreement, Articles 3 and 4.
10. International Energy Agency, 'Net Zero by 2050' (May 2021), https://www.iea.org/reports/net-zero-by-2050 (accessed on 21 February 2024); UK Parliament, 'Accelerating the transition from fossil fuels and securing energy supplies' (Fourth Report of Session 2022-23), at https://publications.parliament.uk/pa/cm5803/cmselect/cmenvaud/109/report.html (accessed on 21 February 2024).
11. UNFCC, 'COP28: What Was Achieved and What Happens Next?' (12 January 2024), https://unfccc.int/cop28.

In this context, various stakeholders – including governments, academics, activists, and the media – have questioned the ECT's role in the energy transition,[12] expressing the concern that it poses an insuperable obstacle for States as they seek to phase out fossil fuels.[13]

This narrative has been fueled by a handful of cases in which the ECT has been used by fossil fuel investors to bring claims in respect of a State's 'phase out' regulations. For example, in *Rockhopper v. Italy*, the UK oil company Rockhopper claimed that the decision to ban offshore drilling breached Italy's obligations under the ECT. The legislation had initially included an exemption for pending permits, and the tribunal found that Rockhopper had done everything required to secure a production concession. However, Italy later removed the exemption and rejected Rockhopper's application. The tribunal found that this reversal constituted an 'immediate and complete deprivation' of Rockhopper's investment, which amounted to an unlawful expropriation under the ECT.[14] The tribunal awarded Rockhopper roughly EUR 240 million in damages.[15]

Notably, the tribunal 'indicate[d] at the very outset that it should not be taken in any way to either criticise or deprecate [Italy's decision to ban offshore drilling] from either a political or environmental standpoint'.[16] The tribunal continued that it:

> Appreciates and is acutely sensitive to the fact that there are strongly-held environmental, civic and political views about offshore production .... However, the outcome of this case passes no judgment whatsoever on the legitimacy or validity of those views. In particular, the Tribunal is at pains to point out that this award is not a 'victory' for one side or the other in that environmental debate, which is of a civic or political character, but rather addresses the legal issue at hand, namely, whether compensation is due to a foreign investor in respect of its investment, based on specific international criteria as contained in a treaty to which Italy was, at the material time, a contracting party.[17]

Three other cases are also cited as examples of challenges to phasing out regulations under the ECT, namely:

12. *See, e.g.*, The Guardian, 'Outrage as Italy Faces Multimillion Pound Damages to UK Oil Firm', 25 July 2021, available at https://www.theguardian.com/business/2021/jul/25/outrage-as-italy-faces-multimillion-pound-damages-to-uk-oil-firm.
13. *See, e.g.*, Hannah Robinson, 'What We Know about the EU's Mysterious Energy Charter Treaty' (21 October 2020) available at https://www.opendemocracy.net/en/can-europe-make-it/what-we-know-about-eus-mysterious-energy-charter-treaty/; The Irish Minister for the Environment, Climate and Communications (Deputy Eamon Ryan), 'Energy Charter Treaty: Statements' (9 November 2023) available at: https://www.oireachtas.ie/en/debates/debate/dail/2023-11-09/34/.
14. *Rockhopper Italia S.p.A., Rockhopper Mediterranean Ltd, and Rockhopper Exploration Plc v. Italian Republic*, ICSID Case No. ARB/17/14, Final Award (23 August 2022), ¶¶ 194, 199.
15. *Rockhopper Italia S.p.A., Rockhopper Mediterranean Ltd, and Rockhopper Exploration Plc v. Italian Republic*, ICSID Case No. ARB/17/14, Final Award (23 August 2022), ¶¶ 215, 292, 335. Italy has filed for annulment: https://www.iareporter.com/articles/icsid-ad-hoc-committee-rules-on-lifting-of-stay-of-enforcement-in-rockhopper-v-italy-case/.
16. *Rockhopper Italia S.p.A., Rockhopper Mediterranean Ltd, and Rockhopper Exploration Plc v. Italian Republic*, ICSID Case No. ARB/17/14, Final Award (23 August 2022), ¶ 6.
17. *Rockhopper Italia S.p.A., Rockhopper Mediterranean Ltd, and Rockhopper Exploration Plc v. Italian Republic*, ICSID Case No. ARB/17/14, Final Award (23 August 2022), ¶ 10.

- Two arbitrations against the Netherlands, brought by German investors RWE and Uniper in respect of the Netherlands' decision to phase out coal-fired power plants by 2030.[18] RWE and Uniper claimed, among other things, that the Dutch regulation failed to provide adequate compensation for the allegedly unexpected change of policy.[19] Both cases have now been discontinued. RWE discontinued the claim following the German court's finding that the 'intro-EU' arbitration was inadmissible.[20] Uniper withdrew its claim as part of its bail-out by the German government.[21]
- An ongoing claim by UK investor Ascent Resources against Slovenia,[22] in which Ascent Resources reportedly claims that Slovenia conducted a 'populist campaign' against its investment, first, by introducing an environmental impact assessment requirement (despite the conclusion of certain expert bodies in Slovenia that one was not required), followed by a complete ban on fracking.[23] Ascent Resources reportedly claims losses in excess of EUR 500 million.[24]

These cases have received widespread negative coverage in the media. For example, The Guardian has criticised '[s]ecretive tribunals [that] allow fossil fuel companies to sue governments for passing laws to protect the environment'[25] and called the ECT 'the disastrous international charter treaty'; 'a secret weapon' of '[f]ossil

18. *RWE AG and RWE Eemshaven Holding II BV v. Kingdom of the Netherlands*, ICSID Case No. ARB/21/4; *Uniper SE and others v. Kingdom of the Netherlands* (ICSID Case No. ARB/21/22). *See* Lisa Bohmer, 'RWE v Netherlands Arbitration is Suspended, Pending Appeal Against German Anti-Arbitration Declaration', *IA Reporter* (15 November 2022) available at: https://www.iareporter.com/articles/rwe-v-netherlands-arbitration-is-suspended-pending-appeal-against-german-anti-arbitration-declaration/.
19. Lisa Bohmer, 'RWE v Netherlands Arbitration is Suspended, Pending Appeal Against German Anti-Arbitration Declaration', *IA Reporter* (15 November 2022) available at: https://www.iareporter.com/articles/rwe-v-netherlands-arbitration-is-suspended-pending-appeal-against-german-anti-arbitration-declaration/.
20. Lisa Bohmer, '[Updated] RWE Requests Discontinuance of Coal Phase-Out ECT Claim Against the Netherlands, in View of German Supreme Court's Ruling on Anti-Intra-EU Arbitration Declarations, *IA Reporter* (2 November 2023) available at: https://www.iareporter.com/articles/rwe-requests-discontinuance-of-coal-phase-out-ect-claim-against-the-netherlands-in-view-of-german-supreme-courts-ruling-on-anti-intra-eu-arbitration-declarations/.
21. Vladislav Djanic, 'Discontinuance Order In Uniper v. Netherlands Surfaces, Revealing That The Tribunal Rejected Request For Costs, Finding No Support For General Rule That Respondent Should Not Bear The Cost Of Withdrawn Claims', *IA Reporter* (6 April 2023) available at https://www.iareporter.com/articles/discontinuance-order-in-uniper-v-netherlands-surfaces-revealing-that-the-tribunal-rejected-request-for-costs-finding-no-support-for-general-rule-that-respondent-should-not-bear-the-cost-of-withdraw/#topic-shortcode-S24736.
22. *Ascent Resources Plc. and Ascent Slovenia Ltd. v. Republic of Slovenia*, ICSID Case No. ARB/22/21.
23. Press Release of Ascent Resources Plc on Arbitration Initiation and Revised Damages Estimate, 15 August 2022; Letter from Enyo Law to Mr Janez Janša et al., 'Notice of Dispute' (23 July 2020); Letter from Enyo Law to Ms Nataša Pintar Gosenca et al., 'Notice of Dispute' (5 May 2022).
24. *Ibid.*
25. The Guardian, 'Outrage as Italy Faces Multimillion Pound Damages to UK Oil Firm' (25 July 2021), https://www.theguardian.com/business/2021/jul/25/outrage-as-italy-faces-multimillion-pound-damages-to-uk-oil-firm.

fuel companies'.[26] The Financial Times, in an opinion piece, referred to the ECT as 'a threat to the UK's net zero ambitions at home and its credibility abroad' and claimed that 'the treaty is increasingly being weaponised by fossil fuel companies in order to sue governments for introducing climate policies'.[27] Other media outlets have criticised the ECT for 'threatening global climate goals', 'increasing the cost of climate change' and 'steal[ing] from developing countries' the funds needed to tackle climate change.[28]

Similar complaints have been voiced by scholars and civil society representatives. For example, a group of over 100 academics sent a letter to the UK Government in February 2023, stating that withdrawal from the ECT is necessary because:

> [t]he ECT can significantly increase the cost of climate action by allowing cases to be brought which compensate investors (including in fossil fuels) for the loss of hypothetical future profits and providing significantly larger amounts of compensation than would be available through domestic courts. There is also evidence that countries are shying away from introducing new legislation for fear of being challenged in claims under the ECT.[29]

ClientEarth has also argued in favour of withdrawal from the ECT on the basis that:

> [t]he fossil fuel industry has used this mechanism more than any other, challenging a wide range of policy measures but critically those designed to protect the environment and climate. And with no cap on compensation pay-outs, fossil fuel companies can sue for billions – creating a catastrophic chilling effect for governments that want to take necessary steps to curb dangerous global heating but fear reprisals by industry.[30]

The UN Intergovernmental Panel on Climate Change (IPCC), in its Sixth Assessment Report on the Mitigation of Climate Change, has recognised the 'potential' of investment agreements 'to increase low-carbon investment in host countries'. But it

26. Cleodie Rickard, 'Fossil Fuel Companies Have a Secret Weapon: Here's How Britain Can Help Take It Away from Them' (13 September 2023), https://www.theguardian.com/commentisfree/2023/sep/13/fossil-fuel-companies-britain-international-charter-treaty.
27. Chris Skidmore, 'Britain Must Leave the Energy Charter Treaty' (5 March 2023) *Financial Times* (Opinion); Mehreen Khan, 'EU Urged to Quit Energy Treaty as Companies Sue over Climate Action' (7 February 2021) *Financial Times*.
28. Euronews, 'Inside the "Secretive" Tribunals Where Fossil Fuel Companies "steal" from Developing Countries' (19 November 2022), https://www.euronews.com/green/2022/11/19/inside-the-secretive-tribunals-where-fossil-fuel-companies-steal-from-developing-countries (quotation marks omitted). *See also* Economic Times, 'UK Fossil Fuel Company Wins £210M from Secretive Tribunal Over Oil Drilling Ban' (5 September 2022), https://economic-times.co.uk/politics/uk-fossil-fuel-company-wins-210m-from-secretive-tribunal-over-oil-drilling-ban/.
29. Academic Letter urging UK Government to exit Treaty that threatens climate action, 9 February 2023, available at https://warwick.ac.uk/fac/soc/law/research/centres/chrp/governance/energycharter/.
30. ClientEarth, The EU must withdraw from the Energy Charter Treaty, 20 September 2022, available at https://www.clientearth.org/latest/news/the-eu-must-withdraw-from-the-energy-charter-treaty/.

has also warned of the 'regulatory chill' that 'may lead to countries refraining from or delaying the adoption of mitigating policies, such as phasing out fossil fuels'.[31]

This criticism has been picked up by the Contracting Parties to the ECT, including as part of the justification for announced withdrawals from the Treaty. For instance, France has voiced a purported concern about the 'incompatibility between the timetables for decarbonisation of the energy sector with the safeguards stipulated in the [ECT]'.[32] It continued that '[t]he threat of [ECT disputes] could limit State[s'] ambitions and lead to "regulatory chill" as regards their low-carbon roll-out policies'.[33] Irish lawmakers referred to the ECT as 'a relic of a fossil fuel past .... [It] represents a bad deal for Ireland and a worse deal for the environment. It offers so-called investment protection to fossil fuel companies meaning they can employ it to slow down the transition to net zero'.[34]

The EU has also been vocal in expressing its alleged climate-related concerns. Over 140 Members of the European Parliament published a statement noting that 'the ECT is a serious threat to Europe's climate neutrality target .... By 2050, cumulative greenhouse gas emissions protected by the ECT, if fossil fuels are not phased out, would be equivalent to one-third of the remaining global Carbon budget for the period 2018-2050'.[35] The European Commission, in recommending a coordinated withdrawal from the Treaty, stated that the ECT 'is largely unchanged since it was agreed in the 1990s and is no longer compatible with the EU's enhanced climate ambition under the European Green Deal and the Paris Agreement'.[36]

## §5.04 THE ECT'S ROLE IN THE ENERGY TRANSITION: IS THE CRITICISM MISPLACED?

As set out in the previous section, the perception that the ECT is fundamentally incompatible with efforts to combat climate change and transition away from fossil fuels is widespread. But is it justified? As set out in further detail below, a proper understanding of the ECT – grounded in the language of the Treaty and relevant case law – reveals that it has a significant positive role to play in the energy transition. In particular, it provides important protections for investors in the clean energy projects that are integral to the global transition effort.

31. IPCC, Climate Change 2022: Mitigation of Climate Change, p. 1499 (2022), https://www.ipcc.ch/report/ar6/wg3/downloads/report/IPCC_AR6_WGIII_FullReport.pdf.
32. French High Council on Climate, Report on the Modernisation of the Energy Charter Treaty (October 2022), available at https://www.hautconseilclimat.fr/wp-content/uploads/2022/10/2022-10-19-TCE_HCC_EN.pdf.
33. *Ibid.*
34. 'Energy Charter Treaty: Statements' (9 November 2023) available at: https://www.oireachtas.ie/en/debates/debate/dail/2023-11-09/34/.
35. Statement on the modernisation of the Energy Charter Treaty, September 2020, available at https://www.euractiv.com/wp-content/uploads/sites/2/2020/09/Statement-on-Energy-Charter-Treaty-ENG_080920.
36. European Commission, European Commission proposes a coordinated EU withdrawal from the Energy Charter Treaty, 7 July 2023, available at https://energy.ec.europa.eu/news/european-commission-proposes-coordinated-eu-withdrawal-energy-charter-treaty-2023-07-07_en.

### [A] The Language of the ECT: An Energy-Agnostic Treaty

Article 2 of the ECT defines its '[p]urpose' in the following terms:

> This Treaty establishes a legal framework in order to promote long-term cooperation *in the energy field*, based on complementarities and mutual benefits, in accordance with the objectives and principles of the Charter.[37]

Notably, the reference to the 'energy field' is broad, without restriction as to the source of energy covered by the Treaty. This reflects a fundamental truth underpinning the ECT: it is *energy-agnostic*. It promotes cooperation – and thus protects investment – with respect to all types of energy, not just fossil fuels.

This point is stated even more clearly in other ECT provisions. For example, Article 1(6) defines the types of '[i]nvestment[s]' that the ECT protects broadly, to include 'any investment associated with an Economic Activity in the Energy Sector'. The concept of 'Economic Activity in the Energy Sector' is defined in Article 1(5), and the Understanding to Article 1(5) provides a list of 'activities [that] are illustrative of Economic Activity in the Energy Sector':

> ***Understanding with respect to Article 1(5)***
>
> (a) ...
> (b) The following activities are illustrative of Economic Activity in the Energy Sector:
>   (i) prospecting and exploration for, and extraction of, e.g., *oil, gas, coal and uranium*;
>   (ii) construction and operation of power generation facilities, including those powered by wind and other *renewable energy sources*;
>   ...
>   (iv) removal and disposal of wastes from energy related facilities such as power stations, including radioactive wastes from ***nuclear power stations***....[38]

In other words, investments in renewable energy and nuclear energy projects are *expressly* referenced as protected investments under the ECT, underlining their potential role as a positive force in the energy transition.

### [B] The ECT in Practice: Significant Protection for Renewable Investors

In light of the energy-agnostic nature of the ECT, it is unsurprising that it has been invoked with regard to a variety of energy investments. While recent cases brought by fossil fuel investors have captured headlines, statistics demonstrate that a considerable *majority* of claims under the ECT have been brought by investors in *renewable* energy projects:

37. ECT, Article 2 (emphasis added).
38. ECT, Understanding with respect to Article 1(5) (emphases added).

- Almost twice as many known claims under the ECT have been brought by renewable energy investors compared to fossil fuel investors. Of the 162 known cases registered as of 1 December 2023, 58.02% relate to renewable energy and 33.3% to fossil fuel investments.[39]
- Renewable energy investors have recovered more damages under the ECT than fossil fuel investors. Of the total EUR 2.37 billion damages awarded under the ECT (excluding the EUR 40 billion *Yukos v. Russia* award[40]), renewable energy investors have recovered roughly EUR 1.3 billion in damages, compared to fossil fuel investors, whose total overall recovery stands at EUR 1 billion.[41]
- Notably, recovery levels for both types of investors under the ECT are low: renewables investors have recovered 5.6%, while fossil fuel investors have recovered 7.7% of the damages claimed.[42]

Viewed in this light, the ECT provides exactly the investment protection that is necessary to transition away from fossil fuels towards clean energy. Indeed, the ECT has been the go-to investment treaty to hold States accountable for the rollback of regulatory incentives extended to attract foreign investment in nascent renewables technology. Spain has been the most frequent respondent in these cases,[43] but investors have also registered renewables claims against Italy, Czechia, France, Germany, Poland, Romania, Ukraine and Bulgaria.[44]

The Spanish experience is well-known and instructive.[45] In 2007, as part of an effort to meet EU-mandated renewable energy targets,[46] Spain enacted a Royal Decree

39. Energy Charter Secretariat, Statistics, available at https://www.energychartertreaty.org/cases/statistics/.
40. *Yukos Universal Limited (Isle of Man) v. Russian Federation*, PCA Case No. 2005-04/AA227, Final Award, 18 July 2014; *Hulley Enterprises Limited (Cyprus) v. Russian Federation*, PCA Case No. 2005-04/AA226, Final Award, 18 July 2014; *Veteran Petroleum Limited (Cyprus) v. Russian Federation*, PCA Case No. 2005-04/AA228, Final Award, 18 July 2014.
41. Energy Charter Secretariat, Statistics, available at https://www.energychartertreaty.org/cases/statistics/. The number excludes the *Yukos v. Russia* award of EUR 40 billion.
42. Energy Charter Secretariat, Statistics, available athttps://www.energychartertreaty.org/cases/statistics/.
43. *See* ECT, List of Cases, available at https://www.energychartertreaty.org/cases/list-of-cases/.
44. *See, e.g., ENERGO-PRO a.s. v. Republic of Bulgaria* (ICSID Case No. ARB/15/19); *EVN AG v. Republic of Bulgaria*, ICSID Case No. ARB/13/17; *ACF Renewable Energy Limited v. Republic of Bulgaria* (ICSID Case No. ARB/18/1); *Encavis AG and others v. French Republic* (ICSID Case No. ARB/22/22); *Erste Nordsee-Offshore Holding GmbH, Strabag SE, Zweite Nordsee-Offshore Holding GmbH v. Federal Republic of Germany* (ICSID Case No. ARB/19/29); *Mainstream Renewable Power Ltd and others v. Federal Republic of Germany* (ICSID Case No. ARB/21/26); *EP Wind Project (Rom) Six Ltd. v. Romania* (ICSID Case No. ARB/20/15); *KELAG-Kärntner Elektrizitäts-Aktiengesellschaft and others v. Romania* (ICSID Case No. ARB/21/54); *Anina Pro Invest Ltd, Core Value Capital GmbH, Core Value Investments GmbH & Co KG Gamma and others v. Romania* (ICSID Case No. ARB/18/19); *Ojeocan Management Ltd v. Republic of Poland* (SCC Case No. 2017/200); *CEF Energia BV v. Italian Republic* (SCC Case No. 2015/158); *Modus Energy International B.V. v. Ukraine* (SCC Case No. 2021/039); *Natland Investment Group NV, Natland Group Limited, G.I.H.G. Limited, and Radiance Energy Holding S.A.R.L. v. The Czech Republic* (PCA Case No. 2013-35).
45. *See further* S Rowe, M Lawry-White and AM Mozetič, '*Renewable Energy Investments –*

establishing a 'Special Regime' for renewable energy projects. The Special Regime extended a number of incentives to investors in renewable energy. This included fixed tariffs that would apply for the entire lifetime of an installation and a grandfathering clause, pursuant to which any subsequent changes to the tariffs would not apply to 'existing installations'.[47] The 2007 Decree followed a series of unsuccessful regulations which had failed to attract sufficient levels of investment in Spain's renewables sector.[48]

The 2007 Decree succeeded where previous regulation had failed: domestic and foreign investment in Spanish renewables soared.[49] The fixed tariffs and grandfathering clause combined to provide a long-term, stable and predictable revenue stream for renewables investors.[50] This was essential for attracting investment into the nascent renewables sector, given that (i) substantial financial support was required to cover the cost of commercialising the relevant technology; (ii) the majority of a renewables project's costs are incurred upfront, at the construction stage, and are therefore fixed and cannot be reduced at a later date; (iii) many investments were supported by project finance loans, and stable and predictable income was required to meet lenders' 'bankability' thresholds; and (iv) renewables projects have long lead-times for investment returns.[51] Spain was proactive in highlighting this aspect of its Special Regime to foreign investors, assuring them that the 2007 Decree aimed to 'preserve the legal security of all investments currently underway, thereby guaranteeing the forecasts under which said investments are to be made'[52] and constituted a 'warranty by law'.[53]

Between 2010 and 2014, however, Spain enacted a series of regulations that dismantled the Special Regime. Among other things, and contrary to the express language of the grandfathering clause, the fixed tariffs were replaced by variable 'special payments', which applied to existing and new installations alike.[54] These 'rollback' measures have given rise to over fifty investment arbitrations against Spain, many of which were brought under the ECT.[55] Investors most commonly complained

*International Protections to Mitigate Risks*', American Investment Council Newsletter (30 November 2021).

46. Directive 2009/28/EC.
47. Royal Decree 661/2007, Articles 36 40(3) and 44(3).
48. *See, e.g., Mathias Kruck, Frank Schumm, Joachim Kruck, Jürgen Reiss and others v. Kingdom of Spain*, ICSID Case No. ARB/15/23, Decision on Jurisdiction, Liability and Principles of Quantum (14 September 2022), ¶ 47.
49. *Ibid.*
50. *See, e.g., Infrastructure Services Luxembourg S.à.r.l. and Energia Termosolar B.V. (formerly Antin Infrastructure Services Luxembourg S.à.r.l. and Antin Energia Termosolar B.V.) v. Kingdom of Spain*, ICSID Case No. ARB/13/31, Award (15 June 2018), ¶¶ 553-554.
51. *Ibid.*
52. *See, e.g., NextEra Energy Global Holdings B.V. and NextEra Energy Spain Holdings B.V. v. Spain*, ICSID Case No. ARB/14/11, Decision on Jurisdiction, Liability and Quantum Principles (12 March 2019), ¶¶ 588-592.
53. *Ibid.*, ¶ 422.
54. *See further* S. Rowe, M. Lawry-White and A.M. Mozetic.
55. *See* Energy Charter Secretariat, Statistics, available at https://www.energychartertreaty.org/cases/statistics/.

and recovered damages on the basis that these regulatory changes completely undermined the economic basis of their investment, breaching their right to fair and equitable treatment (FET) and, in some cases, expropriating their investment.

For example, an ICSID tribunal in *NextEra v. Spain* ordered Spain to pay over EUR 290 million to the claimants on the basis that Spain had frustrated their legitimate expectation to receive the remuneration promised under the 2007 regime in violation of Spain's FET obligations.[56] The tribunal found that Spain's 'regime ... fundamentally and radically changed'.[57] Accordingly, the tribunal held that:

> Claimants were deprived of the security and certainty that, in light of the assurances they had received from Spanish authorities about guaranteeing the legal security of investments underway as well as the forecasts under which the investments were made and affirming legal and regulatory stability, they could have expected. The changes went beyond anything that might have been reasonably expected by Claimants when they undertook their investment.[58]

The vast majority of ECT tribunals have joined the *NextEra* tribunal in finding against Spain and awarding damages to the investor,[59] although some tribunals have found that Spain did not create legitimate expectations for particular investors on the particular facts of the case.[60]

The Spanish cases illustrate how the ECT can be – and has been – used as a powerful tool to support regulations that States have enacted to effect the energy transition (such as Spain's 2007 Special Regime) and protect renewables investments where these regulations are subsequently rolled back by the State, undermining their economic viability.

## §5.05 THE FUTURE OF THE ECT?

The ECT thus has significant potential as a tool to support the energy transition by protecting critical foreign investment in clean technology. Today, however, it is unclear what the future holds for the ECT. While a modernisation effort remains ongoing, a

---

56. *NextEra Energy Global Holdings B.V. and NextEra Energy Spain Holdings B.V. v. Spain*, ICSID Case No. ARB/14/11, Decision on Jurisdiction, Liability and Quantum Principles (12 March 2019), ¶¶ 587ff.
57. *Ibid.*, ¶599.
58. *Ibid.*, ¶599.
59. *See* the Energy Charter Treaty Secretariat, https://www.energychartertreaty.org/cases/statistics/#:~:text=*%20According%20to%20the%20Ministry%20for,for%20a%20new%20incentive%20scheme. *See also* GAR, *Renewables investors to renounce awards against Spain* (6 October 2020), available at https://globalarbitrationreview.com/renewables-investors-renounce-awards-against-spain; *see also* GAR, *Spain offers incentives to end renewables claims* (22 November 2019), available at https://globalarbitrationreview.com/spain-offers-incentives-end-renewables-claims.
60. *See, e.g., FREIF Eurowind Holdings Ltd v. Kingdom of Spain*, SCC Case No. 2017/060, Final Award (8 March 2021), ¶ 525 (finding no breach on the basis that, among other things, Spain 'consult[ed] with lobby groups before implementing the new regulation' and the investor's 'due diligence' at the relevant time suggested that it was 'in fact aware of the likelihood of changes in the remuneration scheme').

spate of announced withdrawals by the EU and its Member States have called the future of the Treaty into question.

### [A] The ECT Modernisation Process

In 2017, the Energy Charter Conference held in Ashgabat, Turkmenistan, launched a discussion on the potential modernisation of the ECT. In late 2019, the Energy Charter Conference approved suggested policy options and established the Modernisation Group. The Modernisation Group launched negotiations between the Contracting Parties, which began in 2020 and continued through 2022.[61]

In June 2022, after fifteen rounds of negotiations, the ECT Modernisation Group published a draft agreement in principle (AIP) on the modernised version of the ECT.[62] Notably, the AIP provides that the driving force behind modernisation efforts was concerns about the ECT's compatibility with the energy transition:

> Contracting Parties recognised the urgent need to effectively combat climate change ... . A number of provisions were introduced that reaffirm the respective rights and obligations of the Contracting Parties under multilateral environmental and labour agreements, such as the UNFCCC, the Paris Agreement and ILO fundamental conventions, as relevant for the energy sector.[63]

The full draft of the modernised ECT was leaked a few months later.[64]

The AIP and the modernised ECT introduce a number of provisions that would appear to advance the goal of increasing the ECT's compatibility with the energy transition, including:

- The AIP introduces an optional carve-out for fossil fuel investments, which would exclude investments in the oil, fuel wood and coal industries, among others, from the ECT's investment-protection regime.[65] The UK and the EU have indicated their intention to opt into the optional carve-out for existing and future fossil fuel-related investments.[66]
- A new stand-alone article reaffirms Contracting States' right to regulate in the interest of legitimate policy objectives, including 'climate change mitigation and adaptation'.[67]
- A new definition of indirect expropriation clarifies, among other things, that it will not generally prohibit 'non-discriminatory measures that are adopted to

61. ECT, available at https://www.energychartertreaty.org/modernisation-of-the-treaty/.
62. ECT, https://www.energycharter.org/fileadmin/DocumentsMedia/CCDECS/2022/CCDEC2022 10.pdf (the 'AIP').
63. AIP, p. 6.
64. Made public by POLITICO Pro on 12 September 2022, *see* https://www.bilaterals.org/IMG/pdf/reformed_ect_text.pdf (the 'leaked ECT').
65. Annex NI of the leaked ECT.
66. AIP, p. 3.
67. New article, p. 31 of the leaked ECT.

protect legitimate policy objectives', including those targeted as 'climate change mitigation and adaptation'.[68]

- Multiple new provisions on 'sustainable development and corporate social responsibility'[69] provide that Contracting Parties 'will promote and adhere' to sustainable and responsible business conduct and will 'not encourage' investment by lowering environment and labour protection laws and standards. The AIP also indicates further strengthened provisions on environmental impact assessments of energy investment projects.

Notably, however, the proposed amendments extend beyond climate concerns and appear to be intended to exclude a broader swathe of claims, including many of the renewables cases that have been successfully brought against a number of ECT Contracting Parties in recent years. For example, the AIP also clarifies that the modernised ECT will exclude arbitrations between investors of EU Member States on the one hand and EU Member States on the other (intra-EU arbitrations).[70]

The 56 ECT Contracting Parties and signatories were expected to vote on the modernised agreement in April 2023. As of December 2023, the vote has not yet taken place and has been postponed indefinitely. In its end-year 2023 report, the Energy Charter Secretariat listed 'finalisation [of the] modernisation process' as a priority for 2024.[71]

### [B] Withdrawal from the ECT and the Sunset Clause

In 2014, Italy commenced its withdrawal from the ECT – which took effect as of 1 January 2016 – following a number of claims arising out of its rollback of renewable energy incentives.[72] Since then, a number of other States have withdrawn, announced their withdrawal, or contemplated withdrawal from the ECT. As of 31 December 2023:

- Three other EU Member States have withdrawn from the ECT, namely, France, Germany and Poland.[73]
- Luxembourg has delivered notification of its withdrawal, which will take effect on 17 June 2024.[74]

68. Article 13(4) of the leaked ECT.
69. AIP, p. 6. *See also* Article 19 of the leaked ECT.
70. *See also* Article 24(3) of the leaked ECT.
71. Energy Charter Secretariat, Report by the Secretary General on the Activities in 2023, CCDEC 2023, 20 November 2023, ¶ 47.
72. Russia terminated the ECT's provisional application in 2009. *See* I. Mironova, 'Russia and the Energy Charter Treaty' Energy Charter Secretariat (7 August 2014), https://www.energycharter.org/what-we-do/knowledge-centre/occasional-papers/russia-and-the-energy-charter-treaty/.
73. Parlement européen (Think Tank, *Briefing*), 'EU Withdrawal from the Energy Charter Treaty' (4 December 2023) available at https://www.europarl.europa.eu/thinktank/fr/document/EPRS_BRI(2023)754632.
74. Energy Charter Secretariat, 'Written Notification of Withdrawal from the Energy Charter Treaty' (30 August 2023), https://www.energycharter.org/media/news/article/written-notification-of-withdrawal-from-the-energy-charter-treaty/; *see also* Energy Charter Secretariat, Written

- Spain, Netherlands, Slovenia, Denmark, Belgium, Portugal and Ireland have each announced their intention to withdraw.[75]

The European Commission proposed a coordinated withdrawal of the EU, its Member States and Euratom from the ECT in July 2023,[76] following a failure to reach the qualified majority required to approve a common position on the modernised ECT (Germany, France, Spain and the Netherlands abstained).[77] This proposal is subject to approval by a qualified majority of the European Council.[78]

The UK is also reportedly reviewing its membership of the ECT.[79]

This series of actual, announced and potential withdrawals raises the question of the status of the ECT and its investment protections post-withdrawal. Does the ECT continue to bind Contracting Parties after they withdraw?

Article 54 of the Vienna Convention on the Law of Treaties ('***VCLT***') provides that a State can withdraw from a treaty if it satisfies any conditions for withdrawal set out in the treaty itself. Article 47 of the ECT provides that States may withdraw after giving a year's notice, during which any new investments will be covered by the ECT.[80] After that year, the 'sunset' clause at Article 47(3) of the ECT is triggered.[81] Any new investments are not protected by the ECT, but existing investments remain protected for twenty years.

It remains to be seen whether withdrawing States will succeed in circumventing the ECT's sunset clause. One potential route that has been suggested [82] is Article 62 of

Notification of Withdrawal from the Energy Charter Treaty (22 March 2023), https://www.energycharter.org/media/news/article/written-notifications-of-withdrawal-from-the-energy-charter-treaty/ (notifications of withdrawal by France, Germany, Poland).

75. GAR, 'Netherlands moves to quit Energy Charter Treaty' (19 October 2022), https://globalarbitrationreview.com/article/netherlands-moves-quit-energy-charter-treaty; Parlement européen (Think Tank, *Briefing*), 'EU Withdrawal from the Energy Charter Treaty' (4 December 2023) available at https://www.europarl.europa.eu/thinktank/fr/document/EPRS_BRI(2023)754632; and Jorge Liboreiro, 'In U-turn, Brussels recommends EU-wide exit from controversial Energy Charter Treaty' *Euronews* (2 July 2023), available at https://www.euronews.com/my-europe/2023/02/07/in-u-turn-brussels-recommends-eu-wide-exit-from-controversial-energy-charter-treaty.
76. European Commission, European Commission proposes a coordinated EU withdrawal from the ECT, News Announcement, 7 July 2023.
77. European commission, Recommendation for a Council Decision on the approval of the withdrawal of the European Atomic Energy Community from the Energy Charter Treaty, 7 July 2023, p. 2.
78. European Commission, European Commission proposes a coordinated EU withdrawal from the ECT, News Announcement, 7 July 2023.
79. ECT, Written notifications of withdrawal from the ECT, https://www.energycharter.org/media/news/article/written-notifications-of-withdrawal-from-the-energy-charter-treaty/.
80. ECT, Article 47(2) ('Any such withdrawal shall take effect upon the expiry of one year after the date of the receipt of the notification by the Depositary, or on such later date as may be specified in the notification of withdrawal.').
81. ECT, Article 47(3) ('The provisions of this Treaty shall continue to apply to Investments made in the Area of a Contracting Party by Investors of other Contracting Parties or in the Area of other Contracting Parties by Investors of that Contracting Party as of the date when that Contracting Party's withdrawal from the Treaty takes effect for a period of 20 years from such date.').
82. *See, e.g.*, Raza Ali, 'VCLT's Article 62: A valid basis for withdrawing from the ECT' (26 December 2022) *Investment Treaty News*, available at https://www.iisd.org/itn/en/2022/12/26/vclts-article-62-a-valid-basis-for-withdrawing-from-the-ect-raza-ali/.

the VCLT. Article 62 provides that a State may terminate or withdraw from a Treaty – and avoid the sunset clause – as a result of a 'fundamental change of circumstances'.[83] There are three conditions that must be met: (*i*) the change of circumstances must have been unforeseen by the parties when the treaty was concluded, (*ii*) the circumstances that changed must have constituted 'an essential basis of the consent' to the treaty, and (*iii*) the change must have 'radically' transformed the 'extent of obligations still to be performed under the treaty'. In a November 2022 Guidance Note, the ECT Secretariat queried whether the Article 62 test could be met by withdrawing States.[84] The Secretariat referred to the International Court of Justice's judgment in *Gabčíkovo-Nagymaros*, where the court did 'not consider that new developments in the state of environmental knowledge and of environmental law can be said to have been completely unforeseen'.[85]

Another option that has been suggested is 'neutralising' the sunset clause through a modification of the ECT by mutual consent.[86] However, Article 42 of the ECT expressly states that any proposed amendments to the ECT must be adopted by the Energy Charter Conference, following which they will be distributed to all Contracting Parties for ratification, acceptance or approval. No modifications can be made absent the agreement of all ECT Contracting Parties. It seems unlikely that this requirement could be met, and certainly not by the withdrawing States alone.

Finally, the European Commission has, of course, taken the view that the ECT – and its sunset clause – have never applied to intra-EU investments.[87] In October 2022, the European Commission proposed a 'subsequent agreement' on the interpretation of

83. VCLT, Article 62 ('1. A fundamental change of circumstances which has occurred with regard to those existing at the time of the conclusion of a treaty, and which was not foreseen by the parties, may not be invoked as a ground for terminating or withdrawing from the treaty unless: (a) the existence of those circumstances constituted an essential basis of the consent of the parties to be bound by the treaty; and (b) the effect of the change is radically to transform the extent of obligations still to be performed under the treaty.

2. A fundamental change of circumstances may not be invoked as a ground for terminating or withdrawing from a treaty: (a) if the treaty establishes a boundary; or (b) if the fundamental change is the result of a breach by the party invoking it either of an obligation under the treaty or of any other international obligation owed to any other party to the treaty.

3. If, under the foregoing paragraphs, a party may invoke a fundamental change of circumstances as a ground for terminating or withdrawing from a treaty it may also invoke the change as a ground for suspending the operation of the treaty.').

84. Energy Charter Secretariat, Sunset Clause (Article 47 of the ECT) in relation to Article 62 of the Vienna Convention on the Law of Treaties (VCLT), 3 November 2022.

85. Gabčíkovo-Nagymaros Project (Hungary/Slovakia), Judgment of 25 September 1997, I.C.J. Reports 1997, ¶ 104.

86. Haris Huremagić, 'Mission Impossible? Implementing *Komstroy* and Modifying the Energy Charter Treaty' (17 November 2021), available at https://voelkerrechtsblog.org/de/mission-impossible/.

87. European Commission, 'Annex to the Communication from the Commission to the European Parliament and the Council, as well as to the Member States on an Agreement between the Member States, the European Union, and the European Atomic Energy Community on the Interpretation of the Energy Charter Treaty', COM(2022) 523 final (5 October 2022), https://eur-lex.europa.eu/resource.html?uri = cellar:3d54cece-4494-11ed-92ed-01aa75ed71a1.0001.02/DOC_2&format = PDF.

the ECT to that effect.[88] The proposed agreement invites the ICSID and SCC Secretariats to refuse to register any new intra-EU claims based on the ECT. No developments regarding this 'subsequent agreement' have been made public since.

## §5.06 CONCLUSION

In short, as the ECT enters its thirtieth year, its future is in question - perhaps unjustifiably so. The Treaty has been subject to significant criticism in recent years from a range of stakeholders, who claim that its provisions are incompatible with the energy transition and broader efforts to combat climate change. However, a careful review of the ECT's provisions and the cases that have been brought to date reveals that the ECT has served as a powerful tool *in support of* the energy transition. In particular, it has protected foreign investors from the rollback of incentives that made their investments in nascent renewables technology viable. It remains to be seen whether the Treaty will survive for another thirty years or whether, instead, it will be modernised in a manner that enhances its compatibility with the energy transition.

88. European Commission, 'Annex to the Communication from the Commission to the European Parliament and the Council, as well as to the Member States on an Agreement between the Member States, the European Union, and the European Atomic Energy Community on the Interpretation of the Energy Charter Treaty', COM(2022) 523 final (5 October 2022), https://eur-lex.europa.eu/resource.html?uri=cellar:3d54cece-4494-11ed-92ed-01aa75ed71a1.0001.02/DOC_2&format=PDF.

# Panel 4 Environmental Footprint of Arbitration Practitioners: Towards Greener Arbitrations?

CHAPTER 6

# Summary of the Panel Discussion

*Urs Weber-Stecher*

## §6.01 INTRODUCTION

The following short chapter summarizes the discussion held with the members of the last panel at the ASA Conference. No introductory speeches were given, but current issues related to the footprint of arbitration practitioners and what actions could be taken by which actors in the arbitration community to move together towards greener arbitration were discussed.[1]

The panel was composed of the following individuals: Lucy Greenwood, arbitrator and founder of the Campaign for Greener Arbitrations;[2] Alison Pearsall, in-house counsel and member of the ASA Users' Council; Jackie van Haersolte-van Hof, Director General of the LCAI;[3] and Florian Mohs, a partner of Pestalozzi's Litigation & Arbitration Group in Zurich. The panel discussion was moderated by Urs Weber-Stecher, an independent arbitrator and member of the ASA Board.

The discussion below assumes that a climate emergency exists and that international arbitrators have a duty to mitigate their impact on the environment. The discussion therefore addressed straightforwardly '*the "what", the "why", the "who" and the "how"*' in relation to the exercising of the practitioner's functions in the field of international arbitration.

The panellists addressed the personal responsibility of everyone involved in arbitration from different angles: from the perspective of the arbitrator, the arbitral institution, the external counsel representing companies in arbitration proceedings and, most importantly, the in-house counsel as the user of arbitration services. The

1. Some footnotes provide further references to aspects that were raised in the discussion or are related to it.
2. Campaign for Greener Arbitrations.
3. The London Court of International Arbitration (LCIA).

discussion focussed on very concrete ways in which each and every arbitration practitioner can contribute to a more environmentally friendly and socially responsible arbitration practice.

## §6.02 DISCUSSION

**Question: Is it enough these days to provide clients with good services, or do clients now also demand that services fulfil certain environmental, social and governance standards?**

From an in-house counsel's perspective, the elements of governance, diversity and inclusion have been considered in the procurement process to date, and in the future, there is a possibility that the elements related to ESG will also be considered as part of the procurement process. The COVID-19 pandemic has had a significant impact on reducing the carbon footprint of work in the legal departments of corporations by suddenly requiring virtual hearings, remote depositions and significantly less travelling. Challenges faced by the teams in adapting to these new practices include the fact that it is not possible to have lawyers and experts in the same room for instructional meetings in complex cases. However, there are also significant benefits to emphasize, such as saving time and money and reducing the carbon footprint, as there is no need to fly in experts and external lawyers for face-to-face meetings. Another advantage is that virtual hearings offer practical benefits as, for example, documents can be displayed simultaneously while all parties can see each other via the screen. Face-to-face meetings for certain key milestones are still essential, but wherever possible, the aim should be to get things done via online platforms.

Also, from the perspective of an arbitration institution, it is not enough just to offer good services. ESG standards must be considered in the context of all professional activities. It is not a one-size-fits-all or one-dimensional discussion. The COVID-19 pandemic, for example, has made life easier in some ways because it has enabled people to do things in a virtual environment. However, there have also been challenges. For example, in virtual presentations on a sensitive topic, it is more difficult to get a feel for the audience, its composition and its reactions to what is being said. Even though there are advantages to communicating with individuals who cannot or should not be travelling, there is the question of the sustainability of this approach in the long term.

During the pandemic, hearings were successfully held with fewer participants. However, if one asks the parties about their wishes for an upcoming hearing, a return to the traditional model can be observed where a room is filled with numerous participants, although ultimately, only a few people are speaking. This observation raises the question of the need for a return to such arrangements. Everyone could focus on becoming more modest and travelling less or trying to combine different tasks that would each require travel into one trip rather than travelling back and forth several times a week. Ultimately, the community needs to find the right balance between the pros and cons of virtual and in-person meetings.

For arbitration practitioners, the importance of building and maintaining trust must be highlighted. It is also referred to as 'social capital' in both in-person and remote interactions. The significance of face-to-face gatherings as opportunities to replenish 'social capital' and the natural tendency of humans to rely on personal relationships for effective communication must be acknowledged. However, this social capital can be easily transferred to the virtual environment once it has been established in person.

In any case it is important to consider the environment in all activities. The Green Pledge for the Campaign for Greener Arbitrations, which began in 2019, is an excellent example of promoting environmental consciousness. The guiding principles of the campaign require arbitration practitioners who sign the Green Pledge to ensure that they minimize the environmental impact of their practice by committing to:[4]

- creating a workspace with a reduced environmental footprint by looking for opportunities to reduce energy consumption and waste;
- corresponding electronically, unless hard copy correspondence is expressly needed in the circumstances, while also being mindful that email has a carbon footprint.
- encouraging the use of videoconferencing facilities as an alternative to travel (including for the purposes of conducting fact-finding or interviews with witnesses);
- avoiding printing, requesting the use of electronic rather than hard copies of documents and promoting the use of electronic bundles at hearings;
- using, where possible, suppliers and service providers who are committed to reducing their environmental footprint (including for the purposes of arranging an arbitration hearing);
- considering and/or suggesting, where appropriate, that witnesses or experts give evidence through videoconferencing facilities rather than attend hearings in person;
- avoiding unnecessary travel and using videoconferencing facilities as an alternative;
- considering and questioning the need to fly at all times and offsetting carbon emissions for any arbitration-related travel.

While the arbitration community has limited ability to tackle the climate crisis single-handedly, they have a duty to lead by example. Moderating individual behaviour alone will not be enough to have a significant impact. Therefore, the community must become aware of the climate crisis and adapt its practices to address it.

Legal professionals are increasingly confronted with regulatory requirements that are influenced by ESG considerations. The trend is for 'soft law' to become 'hard law' and for more and more ESG obligations to be imposed on companies. These requirements will also impact the legal profession when advising their clients, as legal advisers will need to consider all of their clients' obligations.

4. Join us | Campaign for Greener Arbitrations.

The 'G' aspect of ESG, which relates to corporate governance, is already evident in how large corporations pass on their requirements to law firms. Examples include demonstrating equal pay, which is relatively easy for law firms to do, but not achieving equal representation in the partnership. This remains a challenge. For law firms, the 'E' aspect, which relates to the environment, is currently less present, but it is likely to follow in the same vein as the other ESG issues.

The focus of the discussion then shifts to the practical contributions that arbitration can make to environmental issues. While it can be questioned whether a medium-sized arbitration in the Swiss market really requires 20,000 trees to offset the carbon emissions as suggested in international studies[5], it is more interesting to see how the reduced need for printing and travelling due to the COVID-19 pandemic is impacting current data. Many law firms have switched to digital work tools, which has led to a significant reduction in printing. The flip side of the coin is the increased energy consumption associated with digital tools.

Efficient public transport systems are available for travelling and transport within continental Europe. Personal efforts by legal professionals, such as the use of night trains to reduce greenhouse gas emissions, can be observed. While long-haul flights are still necessary for certain destinations, alternative travel options can be used within Europe to minimize the environmental impact.

**Question: Are younger colleagues in law firms happy with the current movement, or would they expect even more changes in terms of sustainability and greener arbitration? And: Can older colleagues be convinced not to fall back into old patterns, and how can they be convinced that it makes sense to stick to the standards achieved or even strive for better standards in terms of greener arbitration?**

Younger colleagues and the younger generation are crucial to the process of making sustainability a priority in the workplace. It is inspiring when children suggest to their parents that they take the train instead of the plane to business meetings, even if it does not always work out. The same attitude can be seen in younger colleagues who are actively involved in creating a sustainable office environment. While it is understandable that the younger generation sometimes wants even more, every little bit counts, and it is important to start somewhere. It is important to put sustainability on the agenda, even if some people may not believe it is necessary. Small actions, such as signing a pledge or adopting a governance code, can help raise awareness and start conversations about sustainability. There is a parallel between gender diversity and sustainability, with more progress to be made in both areas. Although they have been reluctant to talk about sustainability in the past, more and more people are now

5. 'The Campaign for Greener Arbitrations' research [...] revealed that just under 20,000 trees would be required to offset the carbon emissions resulting from a medium-sized arbitration. This is the surprising equivalent of four times the number of trees in Hyde Park or all of the trees in Central Park.' (Herbert Smith Freehills, Inside arbitration: Towards greener arbitrations achieving greater environmental sustainability in the way we conduct arbitrations: an update, 25 February 2021). *See also* Environmental Impact | Campaign for Greener Arbitrations.

realizing the importance of having the conversation and start taking small steps in their own private lives and implement changes towards greener professional practices.

One of the points made in the discussion was that there is a lack of data on the effectiveness of green practices in arbitration, which makes it difficult to convince other colleagues of the need for measures to make arbitration more environmentally friendly. The Green Arbitration Campaign conducted an initial case study in 2019, which showed a significant reduction in carbon emissions and disbursement costs through simple changes such as eliminating printed bundles and reducing the number of flights taken. They reran the numbers on a 'green basis,' factoring in the carbon footprint of an electronic document management system and found a 40-ton reduction in carbon emissions and a 40% reduction in disbursement costs. It is, however, acknowledged that more data is needed on the effectiveness of green practices in arbitration. Other studies are currently being conducted by the Green Arbitration Campaign, as well as electronic case management platform providers. Despite the patchy data on the effectiveness of certain measures to promote green action, it is important to continue to make small changes towards more sustainable practices.

**Question: Does the younger generation in larger law firms have specific expectations of a more sustainable practice that differ from the expectations of older partners?**

The younger generation is the future of law firms, and therefore, it is essential to listen to them and have a dialogue with them. So far, ESG issues have been focusing more on the social governance side than the green side of things. Concerns related to sustainability and green issues are more directed towards clients than the law firms or the arbitration community. There has been a change in attitudes towards remote work and paperless offices due to the COVID-19 pandemic. Even though some partners of the older generation were sceptical about remote work and home office, COVID-19 has proven that remote work is possible to a significant extent. However, there will always be a need for in-person meetings, in particular for team building and educational reasons.

People are social beings and want to interact in private and at social events. More work sessions should be held where people can work together in a relaxed and sociable environment. Even though this is still a brainstorming session, it is important to find a balance between remote working and social interaction to meet the needs of people as social beings.

Also, evidentiary hearings should, as a rule, be in person for the integrity of the arbitration process and the direct personal impression of witnesses and experts. Informal personal exchanges between the formal sessions are also important. This can enable lawyers and parties to get to know each other better and work together more constructively in the further course of the proceedings.

**Question: It is very important for large companies to set sustainability and ESG targets and standards. Is it a challenge for in-house counsel to convince colleagues from the commercial, technical and financial teams that such targets and standards**

**are necessary and could one day be relevant not only for liability reasons but also as part of a successful business strategy?**

The implementation of ESG objectives in a large company is a challenge from the perspective of in-house counsel due to various practical obstacles. Board approval is crucial for the introduction and enforcement of ESG standards in a large company. In addition, organizational structure, lack of time, corporate culture, financial considerations and data collection are some of the biggest challenges that hinder the implementation of sustainability goals. In addition, it is important to have a baseline from which to measure change, and it can be difficult to obtain accurate and reliable data from different business units and regions. Better technology, internal expertise and tools are needed to analyse and identify material information from both an accounting and climate science perspective, which may require new positions. Evolving regulations also require companies to stay on top of and comply with changing laws, which can be a daunting task for in-house counsel. Overall, it takes a comprehensive and coordinated approach by the board, management and in-house counsel to successfully implement ESG goals in a large company.

**Question: Everyone involved in arbitration must strive for higher standards, but the key question is – who should take the lead? If no one takes the lead, everyone expects the others to do something to improve standards and reduce the environmental footprint.**

While institutions such as the LCIA can suggest and work out possible improvements, it is ultimately up to the users of the institution's services to choose the applicable law, the seat, and the institution itself. Therefore, there must be a buy-in from the community that the institution serves for any changes to be effective.

The COVID-19 pandemic triggered an overnight shift towards virtual communication. It is much harder to make changes on green environmental issues, such as limiting the number of participants in evidentiary hearings. While institutions can include provisions about efficiency and effectiveness, it is up to the parties involved to make choices about their lawyers and arbitrators. Ultimately, it is the interplay between the users and their governance codes and boards that determines the support for changes in the industry. Institutions like the LCIA can try to be creative and put something in the rules, but they need support from the community to be effective.

The panellists agreed that in-house counsel will always play an important role when it comes to social, ethical, or environmental risks that may impact the company's bottom line. Part of their role is to manage the ESG agenda and manage the associated regulatory and reputational risks.

**Question: The Scottish Arbitration Center Rules, in their latest version of 2022, referred in Article 23 to the Green Protocol for Arbitral Proceeding developed by the Green Arbitration Campaign, which must be considered. Is this a promising approach?**

One of the purposes of the Green Protocol is to make arbitration conferences more sustainable. The ICCA pursued this approach to sustainability during the last conference. It also wants to make it easier for people who want to change their practices and adopt sustainable approaches without reinventing the wheel. Lucy Greenwood, one of the founders of the Green Arbitration Campaign, is delighted to see the provision in the Scottish Arbitration Rules. One of the key goals of the Campaign is to persuade other institutions to adopt a similar provision when they embark on the next revision of their rules. However, she also expresses sympathy with the idea that individuals should take personal responsibility for their practices rather than blaming institutions. She believes that achieving behavioural change requires strong leadership from those at the top of the profession, who should send a strong message that everyone should consider the environmental impact of their actions. She emphasizes the need to encourage everyone to factor in thoughts about minimizing environmental impact into their thinking, just like they would consider cost implications and other factors related to access to the arbitration process.

**Question: Is it necessary to have national legislators impose obligations on the legal professionals directly or indirectly via the clients which will then transfer from them to the law firms? Or would the initiative also be taken without such legal obligations?**

The legal advisors should make a change out of their own motivation. But more regulations or laws are not necessary. There is a link between efficiency and sustainability. Any steps taken by institutions or professionals towards efficient case handling (tools such as limited document disclosure, definition of issues to be determined, coordination of expert evidence) address environmental concerns at the same. However, case management issues are often addressed reluctantly at the beginning of an arbitration, even though, for instance, the ICC Rules prescribe such an approach. Institutions have begun to provide checklists for efficient case management conferences, but it is ultimately up to individual counsel and their clients to adopt them. It is the responsibility of counsel to raise awareness of sustainability issues in litigation situations, and good lawyers can persuade their clients to follow their advice. Even if the decision ultimately lies with the client, advisers have an important role to play in promoting sustainable dispute resolution practices.

The question arises as to whether it makes sense to regulate behavioural changes such as those discussed in this session. Instead, so-called 'nudges' could be used to encourage people to change their behaviour. 'Nudging' is a concept from behavioural economics in which people are encouraged to change their behaviour in a certain direction by influencing their decision-making process without forcing them to do so. Greenwood cites the Green Protocol as an example of how people are encouraged to adopt a more environmentally friendly arbitration process.

When the Green Protocols were first discussed, there was a debate about whether they should be mandatory or voluntary. After a six-month consultation period, the authors concluded that making them mandatory would put people off while making them voluntary and more detailed would be more effective. Feedback on the Green

Protocols has been positive, and people find them useful because they can decide for themselves which parts they want to incorporate into their practice and which they want to leave out, taking into account their specific circumstances.

It is crucial to empower people to make their own decisions because not every arbitration is the same. Everyone involved in the arbitration process should make the decision to adopt the Green Protocols. In summary, rules should not be imposed, but rather, people should be encouraged to make greener choices.

Even if the change of mindset should come from each individual, a wave of regulation is coming towards companies that will require reporting, especially from an in-house counsel perspective. Specifically, the Corporate Sustainability Reporting Directive (CSRD) and SEC Climate-Related Disclosure Rules[6] will require reporting on Scope 3 emissions, which are upstream and downstream emissions along the company's entire value chain. This means that law firms could be considered service providers in the supply chain, and their emissions could constitute Scope 3 emissions. Given the SEC Rules' requirements for public companies to report on their climate-related risks, emissions, net-zero transition plans, and Scope 3 emissions, the challenge will be how to evaluate and measure these. This would be a major obligation for companies, especially since private suppliers may not be subject to SEC disclosures, and supply chains are multi-layered, requiring detailed information on suppliers' suppliers. There is also a risk of double counting if there are different approaches to calculating emissions. Companies will need more guidance on these issues, but they are coming, and it is important to prepare for them.

Identifying the carbon footprint of international arbitration is a difficult task, and although the team of the Campaign for Greener Arbitrations ran a case study four years ago, they are currently working hard to update and refine it. A team at Dechert put an interesting proposal forward that suggests using carbon emission scorecards at the end of an arbitration. Each side would keep a note of its carbon impact in the arbitration, and a scorecard would be presented before the tribunal when it comes to determining costs. The losing party would then work out the requirements to offset the arbitration costs based on the assumption that it should not have been brought in the first place. It is a radical suggestion but nevertheless a creative proposal with a good intention.

After the discussion with the panellists, two questions were asked by the Audience.

**Question: All arbitration practitioners are there for the users because they are their clients.**

The questioner's personal experience is that medium-sized, small, but also large companies have learnt that they are very efficient when they hold meetings via Zoom or MS Teams and when they do not have to travel, or at least to a much lesser extent, which has led them to expect a high level of efficiency from the lawyers or arbitrators as well. She asks the panellists what their experiences have been and whether their

6. CSRD and SEC Reporting Requirements: What's New for 2024 and Beyond | Intelex Blog.

clients, users and parties in arbitration proceedings expect them as arbitrators or lawyers to be more efficient in terms of travel costs.

From the perspective of an arbitration institution, there is no one-size-fits-all. There are situations where both parties see extensive travelling and face-to-face attendance as essential to the development of the case. If both parties favour in-person meetings, this preference is difficult to overcome despite efforts to promote alternative approaches.

Rather than relying solely on virtual platforms such as Zoom and MS Teams, it is important to put the topic of remote procedures on the agenda and open it up for discussion. While video conferencing can be efficient and suitable for certain aspects of proceedings, interpersonal contact is also important. Each party involved in the arbitration has a say in the decision-making process, making it a collective rather than an individual decision.

From the external lawyer's perspective, it also depends on the client relationship. The COVID-19 pandemic has shown that travelling can be reduced or avoided altogether, particularly in the case of repeat clients or ongoing major cases, and that communication via online platforms is often sufficient. It would be rather difficult to engage new legal counsel without meeting them in person first. However, there is no definitive answer to the question of whether remote or face-to-face meetings are better, as this always depends on the specific circumstances of the individual case.

The minimum that all parties should be able to expect from their arbitrators is that they are technologically competent and efficient. Many discussions about greener arbitration centre on efficiency and the general avoidance of waste that arbitrators should strive for.

**Question: The arbitration community is caught between responsibility for the environment, social aspects, employment, etc. Younger generations, who have had limited interaction with clients and partners due to the COVID-19 pandemic, lack training and networking opportunities. These aspects should not be neglected in the pursuit of efficiency. The panellists are asked to what extent this is an active consideration for them.**

For the LCIA, as an institution offering training events, this is an important and active consideration, as virtual events have resulted in people participating from regions and backgrounds that would never have been able to travel to these events. The same could be observed with hearings, as virtual hearings via Zoom offer the opportunity to include many people who would otherwise not be able to attend. If the training component is taken into account when deciding how to conduct a hearing, the client should ultimately be aware of this fact. The participation of many people in in-person hearings for training purposes may not be in the client's best interest and should be explicitly addressed in advance.

In a way, virtual hearings have also increased the number of client visits for the younger team members, as they have client visits every day, perhaps several a day, via video call. Before, when all meetings were physical, they might attend one meeting a week. Even in larger law firms, evidentiary hearings are not held every day, and virtual hearings allow for greater participation. However, the question then arises as to what role they should play and what contribution they should make apart from simply listening.

It is important to take a holistic approach and consider all the aspects mentioned above. And the carbon footprint was never an issue until about four years ago. It's very inspiring to see how the conversations have evolved from never talking about it to in-depth panel discussions like this one. Nevertheless, in addition to these ESG aspects, aspects such as the training of younger colleagues in a team have to be taken into account when making decisions about arbitration proceedings. So, this tension does exist.

## ASA SPECIAL SERIES*

1. *Le nouveau droit suisse de l'arbitrage international*, 1989.
2. *The New Swiss Law on International Arbitration*, 1990.
3. Michael E. Schneider (ed.), *Verträge und Schiedsverfahren im europäischen Umbruch*, 1990.
4. *Dispute Resolution on International Markets*, 1993.
5. *Investing in Eastern-European Countries – And Arbitration*, 1993.
6. Marc Blessing (ed.), *Objective Arbitrability – Antitrust Disputes – Intellectual Property Disputes*, 1994.
7. *Profiles of ASA Members (1994)*, 1994.
8. Marc Blessing (ed.), *The Arbitration Agreement: Its Multifold Critical Aspects*, 1994.
9. Marc Blessing (ed.), *The New York Convention of 1958*, 1996.
10. *Profiles of ASA Members (1998)*, 1998.
11. *Arbitration of Sports-Related Disputes*, 1998.
12. Pierre Karrer (ed.), *International Arbitration Do's and Don'ts*, Second Edition, 1998.
13. Pierre Karrer (ed.), *The Claims Resolution Process on Dormant Accounts in Switzerland*, 2000.
14. *Profiles of ASA Members (2000)*, 2000.
15. Pierre Karrer (ed.), *Arbitral Tribunals or State Courts: Who Must Defer to Whom?*, 2001.
16. Pierre Karrer (ed.), *Glossary of Arbitration and ADR Terms and Abbreviations*, First Edition, 2001.
17. Pierre Karrer (ed.), *International Arbitration Do's and Don'ts*, Third Edition, 2001.
18. Pierre Karrer (ed.), *Conflicts of Interest in International Commercial Arbitration*, 2001.
19. *Profiles of ASA Members (2002)*, 2002.
20. Gabrielle Kaufmann-Kohler & Viviane Frossard (eds), *Arbitration in Banking and Financial Matters*, 2003.
21. Pierre Karrer (ed.), *International Arbitration Do's and Don'ts*, Forth Edition, 2004.
22. Gabrielle Kaufmann-Kohler & Blaise Stucki (eds), *The Swiss Rules of International Arbitration*, 2004.
23. *Profiles of ASA Members (2005)*, 2005.
24. Gabrielle Kaufmann-Kohler & Alexandra Johnson (eds), *Arbitration of Merger and Acquisition Disputes*, 2005.
25. Pierre Karrer (ed.), *International Arbitration Do's and Don'ts*, Fifth Edition, 2005.
26. Markus Wirth (ed.), Best Practices in International Arbitration, 2006.

* Volumes 47 and onward are published by Wolters Kluwer.

27. Pierre Karrer (ed.), Glossary of Arbitration and ADR Terms and Abbreviations, Second Edition, 2006.
28. Pierre Karrer (ed.), Glossary of Arbitration and ADR Terms and Abbreviations, Third Edition, 2008.
29. Markus Wirth (ed.), *The Resolution of the Dispute, from the Hearing to the Award*, 2007.
30. Michael E. Schneider & Joachim Knoll (eds), *Performance as a Remedy: Non-Monetary Relief in International Arbitration*, 2011.
31. Pierre Karrer (ed.), *International Arbitration Do's and Don'ts*, Sixth Edition, 2009.
32. Pierre Karrer (ed.), *Glossary of Arbitration and ADR Terms and Abbreviations*, Fourth Edition, 2009.
33. *Profiles of ASA Members (2009)*, 2009.
34. Anne K. Hoffmann (ed.), *Protection of Foreign Investments through Modern Treaty Arbitration: Diversity and Harmonisation*, 2010.
35. Markus Wirth, Christina Rouvinez & Joachim Knoll (eds), *Search for "Truth" in Arbitration: Is Finding the Truth What Dispute Resolution Is About?*, 2011.
36. Elliott Geisinger & Guillaume Tattevin (eds), *Advocacy in International Commercial Arbitration*, 2013.
37. Daniele Favalli (ed.), *Sense and Non-sense of Guidelines, Rules and Other Para-regulatory Texts in International Arbitration*, 2015.
38. Pierre Tercier (ed.), *Post Award Issues*, 2012.
39. **Not published.**
40. Philipp Habegger, Daniel Hochstrasser, Gabrielle Nater-Bass & Urs Weber-Stecher (eds), Arbitral Institutions under Scrutiny, 2013.
41. Elliott Geisinger & Elena Trabaldo de Mestral (eds), *Sports Arbitration: A Coach for Other Players*, 2014.
42. Bernhard Berger & Michael E. Schneider (eds), *Inside the Black Box: How Arbitral Tribunals Operate and Reach Their Decisions*, 2013.
43. Elliott Geisinger (ed.), *Confidential and Restricted Access Information in International Arbitration*, 2016.
44. Nathalie Voser (ed.), *10 Years of Swiss Rules of International Arbitration*, 2014.
45. Domitille Baizeau & Frank Spoorenberg (eds), *Arbitrators' Initiative: When, Why and How Should It Be Used?*, 2016.
46. Sebastien Besson & Harold Frey (eds), *Expert Evidence: Conflicting Assumptions and How to Handle Them in Arbitration*, 2020.
47. Andrea Meier & Christian Oetiker (eds), *Arbitration and Corruption*, 2021.
48. Felix Dasser (ed.), *Clear Path or Jungle in Commercial Arbitrators' Conflict of Interest?*, 2021.
49. Elliott E. Geisinger, Christoph Müller, Andrea Menaker & Sabrina Pearson-Wenger (eds), *Good Faith in International Arbitration: Myth, Reality, Label … or All of the Above?*, 2024.
50. Urs Weber-Stecher & James Menz (eds), *ESG and Disputes: Flash in the Pan or Game Changer?*, 2024.